ES OF THE
SH SAINTS

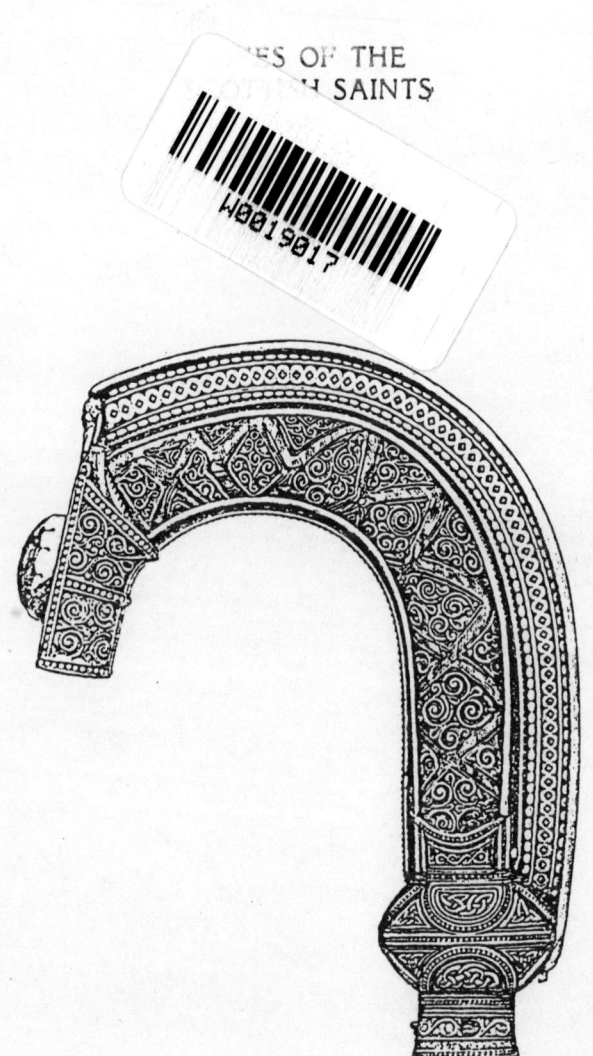

LIVES OF THE SCOTTISH SAINTS

The lives of Saints
Columba, Servanus, Margaret, and Magnus

translated by
W. M. Metcalfe D.D.

Published in 1990 by Llanerch Enterprises.
Cover design: the Monymusk reliquary; frontis-
piece and above, St. Filian's crosiers, drawn by J.
Romilly Allen. Metcalfe's translations were first
published by Alexander Gardner at Paisley, 1895.

CONTENTS

Of the Lives here translated, one - Turgot's Life of St. Margaret - is undoubtedly primitive. It is the only ancient Life of that Saint in existence, with the exception of a shorter one, printed by Surius (1618), which is evidently an abridgement of it. Ciumine's Life of St. Columba is the oldest Life of the Apostle of the Northern Picts which we possess, and must have been written within sixty years of his death (597), but whether it is the primitive Life is somewhat doubtful. Adamnan mentions other writings as among his sources of information, and cites an incident which he says he found in a writing, and of which no mention is made by Cuimine. It may be, however, that these writings were not biographies, but such works as the Amhra, or panegyric, composed by a contemporary of St. Columba, or narratives of particular incidents in the life of the Saint.... The Life of St. Magnus was originally written in Latin by a certain Master Robert, who seems to have been an Orkneyman. From Latin it was translated into Icelandic. Originally it would seem to have been used as a homily or sermon... Lastly, the Life of St. Servanus, though curious, is for the most part fiction, and was evidently written to extol the virtues and greatness of the Saint..... All the Lives with a single exception - that of St. Margaret - abound in miracles. For the most part they are miracles of healing, though a number of them are miracles wrought on nature. The miracles themselves may be nothing, but the details which surround them are authentic, and are therefore of value as to the social condition of the inhabitants of Great Britain and Ireland, and of their religious tenets and practices.

LIFE OF COLUMBA.

BY

CUIMINE THE FAIR.

LIFE OF COLUMBA.

CHAPTER I.

The Nativity of Columba. An Angel appears to his Mother bearing a Mantle Adorned with Flowers.

THE nativity of Columba, sprung from a nation of saints for the salvation of many, is known to have had its beginning on this wise : One night between his conception and his birth, an angel of the Lord appeared to his mother in dreams, and standing beside her gave her a mantle of marvellous beauty, on which, sooth to say, the lovely colours of every flower seemed to be depicted. After a little, however, he demanded it back, took it from her hands, and raising it, spread it out, and sent it away through the empty air. But she, terrified at the mantle being taken from her, then addressed the man of venerable mien : " Why takest thou away from me the delightful mantle so soon ? " He immediately replied : " Because this cloak is of such exceeding honour that it can no longer be kept with thee." At these words, the woman saw the aforesaid mantle recede further and further from her in its flight, and as it grew in size she beheld it exceed in breadth the plains, and surpass in extent the mountains and wooded valleys. At the same time she heard the following words : " O woman, be not grieved, for to the man to whom thou art bound in the bonds of wedlock, thou art about to bear a son of like beauty, who will be numbered among the prophets of the Lord as one of them ; he is predestinated by God to be the leader of innumerable souls to the heavenly land." On hearing this the woman awoke.

CHAPTER II.

A Globe of Fire appears over the Face of Columba.

AFTER the birth of the child, a priest, a man of blameless life, to whose care the blessed youth had been confided, on returning home from church, after Mass, found his whole house lit up with a bright light, and saw a globe of fire resting over the face of the sleeping child. As soon as he beheld it he shook with fear, and lay prostrate on the ground in amazement, perceiving that the grace of the Holy Spirit was poured out upon the child from above.

CHAPTER III.

An Angel His Companion.

ON a certain occasion the Saint, while a young man, went to visit the holy Bishop Finnian, his master, who was then an old man. S. Finnian, when he saw him approaching, beheld likewise an angel of the Lord acting as his companion on the journey, and made known the fact to certain brethren who were standing by, saying : " Behold, see now S. Columba coming ; he has been deemed worthy to have an angel of the Lord as the companion of his journey."

CHAPTER IV.

He Turns Water into Wine.

IN those days the Saint crossed over into Britain with twelve disciples and fellow soldiers. He arrived on a certain holy day, as his holy teacher and bishop Finnian was celebrating Mass, when it chanced that no wine could be found for the sacrificial mystery. On hearing the ministers at the altar complaining of this among themselves, he took a pitcher, and went to the fountain, in order that as a deacon he might draw spring water for the holy ministries of the Eucharist. The water being drawn, he said to the ministers: "You have now wine, which the Lord has sent for the celebration of his mysteries." On this being known, the holy Bishop with the ministers gave exceeding thanks to God. But the holy youth was wont to ascribe this miracle not to himself but to Bishop S. Finnian.

––––

CHAPTER V.

He Consecrates Aidan King, and foretells future things concerning his Son.

AT another time the holy man, while staying in the Island of Hynba (Eilean-na-Naoimh), one night, when in an ecstacy of mind, saw an angel of the Lord sent unto him, who held in his hand the glass book of the ordination of kings. This book he received from the hand of the angel, and began to read. Refusing to ordain Aidan king as he was directed (for he loved his brother more), the angel suddenly stretched forth his hand and smote the Saint with a whip, the mark of the bruise whereof remained on his side all the days of his life. He also addressed to him this word: "Know for certain that I am sent by God, in order that thou mayest ordain Aidan king, which if thou wilt not do, I will smite thee again." The angel of the Lord giving him the same things in charge concerning the ordination of Aidan on three consecutive nights, the Saint sailed over to the Island of Iona, and Aidan coming thither, he ordained him king. Moreover, during the words of ordination, he foretold the future of his sons, and grandsons, and great-grandsons, and laying his hand upon his head, ordained and blessed him, and spake forth these words: "Believe unhesitatingly, O Aidan; none of thine adversaries shall be able to resist thee, until thou first act unjustly towards me and my posterity. Tell these words to thy sons, lest they lose the kingdom. Because if they hearken not, the scourge which, because of thee I have endured from the angel of God, will be turned against them." And so it came to pass, for transgressing the commands of the man of God, they lost the kingdom.

CHAPTER VI.

He sees the soul of a monk received into Heaven.

ON another occasion, when staying in the island of Iona, the holy man saw a monk, who was fruitful in good works, reduced to the last extremity. When he visited him in the hour of his departure, the man of God, after standing for a little beside his couch, blessed him, and then quickly left the house, being unwilling to witness the death of him who at that moment was passing from among them. Then, indeed, the holy man, while walking in the court of his monastery, with his eyes fixed on heaven, was astonished and greatly amazed. One of the brethren, who at the time was alone with him, ventured to ask the cause of his amazement, when the Saint replied: "Just now I saw the holy angels warring against the opposing powers, and I give thanks to Christ, our Judge, because the victorious angels have received the soul of this pilgrim. But I beseech thee, that while I live, thou wilt reveal this secret to no one."

CHAPTER VII.

The Death of Saint Brendan revealed to him.

LIKEWISE on a certain day at the first dawn, the Saint called to him his servant, Diormit, and addressed him on this wise: "Let the services of the Holy Eucharist be at once prepared; for to-day is the natal day of the blessed Brendan." "Wherefore," said the servant, "orderest thou such things; for no messenger from Ireland has announced his death." "Go," replied the Saint, "obey my order; for during the night I saw the heavens suddenly open and choirs of angels, by whose bright and surpassing glory the whole world was in that moment illuminated, descend to meet the soul of S. Brendan.

CHAPTER VIII.

The Death of S. Columban, Bishop in Leinster, revealed.

ON another day, again, when the brethren were about to set out to their manual labour, the Saint, on the contrary, ordered the day to be spent in rest, the rites of the Holy Oblation to be prepared, and some addition to be made to their dinner. "I must needs celebrate," he said, "the mysteries of the Holy Eucharist for the holy soul which was last night carried among the angels." The brethren obeyed, spent the day in rest, and went with the holy Abbot to the Church as on a holy day. During the sacred mysteries of the Holy Sacrifice, the Saint said, "To-day prayer must be made for the holy Bishop Columban." Then understood the brethren who were standing by, that Columban, Bishop of the people in Leinster, the dear friend of Columba, had departed to the Lord. A short time after, some persons coming from the province of Leinster brought tidings that the Bishop died on the night the Saint said.

CHAPTER IX.

Columba fights with demons.

NOW the Saint sought a place among the woods more remote from men and suitable for prayer. And there, when on a certain day he was praying, he suddenly saw before him an exceedingly black host of demons fighting with iron spits, who, as had been revealed to the holy man by the Spirit, were desirous of assailing his monastery and slaying many of the brethren with darts. But he fought against them, and so on both sides the battle was waged during the greater part of the day. But though innumerable, and he one, they were unable to overcome him, till at last the angels of God came to his aid, and through fear of them the demons fled from the place, as the Saint himself afterwards told the brethren.

CHAPTER X.

While staying in Iona he comes by the help of an Angel to the relief of a brother who is falling from the top of a house in Ireland.

AT another time, when the man of God was sitting in his hut writing, his countenance was suddenly changed, and he cried out from a pure heart, saying: "Help! help!" Two brethren, who were standing at the door, asked the reason for this sudden cry; and the man of God gave them the following answer: "I commanded the angel of the Lord, who was just now standing in our midst, to go quickly to the help of one of the brethren who was falling from the roof of a house which is being built." And the Saint immediately added: "Wonderful, indeed, and almost indescribable is the swiftness of the angelic flight; equal, I should think, to the speed of lightning. For that heavenly being who but now flew hence from us to that man as he was beginning to fall, came up, as if in the twinkling of an eye, and supported him before he touched the earth; nor did he feel any shock. How amazing, I say, and how timely the aid, which swifter than a word could be rendered so quickly over so many intervening lands and seas."

CHAPTER XI.

He converses with Angels.

ON a certain occasion, on one of the days when the brethren were assembled together, the Saint of God, Columba, said to them: "To-day I wish to go alone to the western plain of our island; but none of you follow me." They complied with his

request, and he went out alone as he wished ; but a certain
brother, a crafty spy, following another path, hid himself on
the top of a hill, anxious to spy out what he might and did
see, but not without the permission of God, who was magnify-
ing his Saint. For he saw him standing on a hill and praying
with his hands opened out to heaven, and lifting up his eyes
on high. Wonderful to say : lo ! a marvellous sight suddenly
appeared. Straightway holy angels, clothed in white raiment,
flew towards the holy man with wondrous speed, and began to
stand around him as he prayed, and joined in intercourse with
the blessed Saint ; but as if conscious of him who was spying
them, they flew back on high. The blessed man, after the
angelic meeting, betook himself to the monastery, and, the
brethren being assembled, sought for him who was guilty of
the transgression with a stern reproof. He, then, who knew
within himself that he was the inexcusable transgressor,
confessed his guilt and on bended knees prayed for pardon ;
and the Saint leading him aside, charged him, as he knelt,
with a heavy threat to tell no man during his life-time what
he had seen. For a time the brother obeyed, but after the
Saint's death, he related with many protestations to the
brethren what he had seen. Moreover the scene of this
angelic assembly is called to this day the Mount of the Angels.

CHAPTER XII.

A ball of fire rises from his head.

MOREOVER, on another occasion, four brethren came from
Ireland for the sake of visiting S. Columba, who was then
residing in the Island of Hynba (Eilan-na-naoimh). With
one consent they besought the Saint with prayers to celebrate
the Sacred Mysteries ; which also he did one Lord's Day.
But after the reading of the Gospel they saw a certain ball
fiery and very bright, blaze from the crown of the holy
Columba's head, while he stood before the altar consecrating the
Sacred Oblation, and beheld it rise upwards, in the form of a
column, until the same Sacred Mysteries were ended.

CHAPTER XIII.

He enjoys celestial visions during three days.

LIKEWISE, on another occasion, when staying in the same
island, the grace of the Holy Spirit was abundantly and
incomparably poured out upon the holy man, and dwelt with
him in a marvellous manner for the space of three days, so
that for three days and three nights he neither ate nor drank,
nor permitted any one to approach him, but remained in his
house, which was shut up and filled with celestial brightness.
At night rays of surpassing brilliancy were seen to burst from
the house through the chinks in the doors and through the
key-holes, and spiritual songs were heard being chanted by
him, and songs before unheard.   And as he afterwards openly
confessed, he was deemed worthy to learn in that place many
things, both obscure things of the Scriptures and mysteries
unknown to men.

CHAPTER XIV.

He relieves the want of a poor man by a spit he blessed.

ON one occasion there came to the Saint a certain peasant
who was very poor, complaining bitterly that he had not anything wherewith to feed his wife and little ones. Sympathizing
with him, the merciful servant of God said : " Poor man !
Take a stake from the neighbouring wood and bring it to me
quickly." He obeyed, and went and brought one. And the
Saint taking it, sharpened it into a spit, and with his own
hand blessed it and gave it to him, saying : " Watch carefully
over it, it will hurt neither man nor cattle, but only beasts and
game and fish, and so long as thou keepest it, there will be no
want whatever of venison in thy house." On hearing this the
poor man returned to his home rejoicing ; he also fixed the
spit in remote parts of the country which the beasts of the
forest were in the habit of frequenting, and when the night
was passed, went with the first dawn of day to visit it, and

found a stag impaled upon it. But why say more? Not a day passed but the stake caught a buck, a doe, or some other animal. His whole house, as it were, was overflowing with the flesh of wild animals. But not many days after, his foolish wife, overcome by the persuasion of the devil, spake thus to him : " Take the stake from the ground ; for if any of the men or domestic cattle should be killed upon it, thou and I with our children will be led captive or reduced to slavery." " It will not be so," replied the husband ; " for the Saint of God has interdicted it from hurting man or beast." Nevertheless, yielding to his wife, he took the stake out of the field, and placed it beside the wall of his house, when immediately his house dog, running against it, died. On this his wife again said : " One of thy sons will fall upon the stake and die." At this the husband removed it from beside the wall, and carrying it into the wood, placed it among thick bushes, so that it might hurt no one. But when he returned on the following day, he found that a goat had fallen upon it. Removing it thence, he hid and fixed it under water. But revisiting it another day, he found a huge salmon, which he was hardly able to carry alone, impaled upon it. Then he placed the stake upon the roof, when a crow flying by chance against it, was killed. Whereupon the poor man, who was now prosperous, led astray by the counsel of his wife, took the stake from the roof, seized his axe, cut it into many pieces, and threw it into the fire, and immediately became poor.

CHAPTER XV.

He is suffused with Heavenly Light in the Church.

ONE winter night S. Fernaus entered the Church alone to pray, and was devoutly praying at a certain seat. S. Columba, ignorant of this, entered the church a little after for the same purpose, and along with him there entered a golden light, which descended from heaven and filled the whole church. Moreover, the heavenly light filled also the chapel, though it was shut off, where Fernaus was lying hid in great alarm; and as no man can look at the summer sun at noontide with steady unblinking eyes, so also Fernaus could not endure that heavenly splendour. At length having seen the lightning brilliancy no strength remained in him. After a short prayer, however, S. Columba left the church, and on the morrow he called Fernaus to him and addressed him in these consoling words : " O my child, last night thou didst that which was pleasing in the sight of God in bending thine eyes down to the earth for fear of the light. For if thou hadst not so done, thine eyes would have been blinded ; but while I live, take care to keep this vision secret."

CHAPTER XVI.

The Life of Columba is prolonged in answer to the Prayers of the Church.

ON another occasion, also, when the man of God was staying in the Island of Iona, his face glowed with a sudden joyfulness, and lifting his eyes to heaven he rejoiced greatly ; but after a little he became sad. Two brethren, however, who were standing at the door inquired the reason of this sudden joy and the following grief. To whom the Saint replied : " Go in peace. I may not tell you." But when they were too troublesome to him concerning this occurrence, he said : " If you will keep it secret, I will tell you, for I love you." And when they gave their word, he spoke thus to them : " Up to the present day thrice ten years of my pilgrimage in Britain have been fulfilled. Moreover, I have asked from the Lord that in the end of this thirtieth year I might pass away and be with Him. And this was the cause of the joy concerning which ye trouble me. I also saw the holy angels coming to meet my soul as it was about to leave the body. But lo ! they stand afar off, being suddenly held back and not suffered to approach nearer, because He who granted that what I besought should happen on this day, hearkening to the prayers of many churches concerning me, has changed more quickly than I can tell; for in answer to the prayers of the churches, it has been granted by the Lord that four years from this day shall be added to my continuance in the flesh. Now this delay was the cause of my grief. But when these four years are ended, I shall joyfully pass to the Lord by a sudden death."

CHAPTER XVII.

He predicts the Hour of his Death; and blesses Iona.

ACCORDING therefore to these words the man of God lived in the flesh for four years more, which being ended, one day in the month of May, infirm with age and conveyed in a waggon, he went to visit the brethren who were labouring in the fields and began to address them as follows: "During the Easter festival, in the month of April just past, I earnestly desired to pass away to Christ, but that the festival of joy might not be changed for you into sorrow, I preferred to delay the day of my departure longer." At these words the brethren were exceeding sorrowful. But the man of the Lord, as he sat in the vehicle, turned his face towards the East, and blessed the island with the islanders who dwelt therein, and from that day there was no viper in it hurtful to man or beast. At length after the words of benediction, the Saint was borne back to his monastery.

CHAPTER XVIII.

He sees an Angel.

BUT when a few days were passed, while the solemnities of the Mass were being celebrated according to custom on the Lord's Day, suddenly, his eyes being lifted up, the face of the blessed Columba was seen to be overspread with a bright glow. At the same moment he alone beheld an angel of the Lord hovering above within the walls of the oratory. For this was the cause of that sudden joy, concerning which when those present inquired, the Saint made to them this reply : " Wonderful and incomparable is the subtilty of the angelic nature ! For lo ! an angel of the Lord sent for the safe-keeping of some one dear to God, looking down upon us within the church and giving his benediction, has returned again through the roof of the church, and left no trace of such exit." These things the Saint said signifying them concerning himself; nevertheless at the time the brethren knew it not; but afterwards they understood.

CHAPTER XIX.

He indicates the Day of his Death to Diormit.

ACCORDINGLY the holy man at the end of the same week, that is on the Sabbath day (*i.e.*, our Saturday), privately called his servant Diormit to him, and thus spake : " In the Sacred Writings this day is called Sabbath, which, being interpreted, is Rest. And truly to me this day is a Sabbath, because to me it is the last day of life, in which, after the afflictions of my labours, I take my rest, and on the coming Lord's day night, shall go the way of my fathers. For already Christ invites me, and so it is revealed to me by Him." At this the servant was much grieved, but was consoled by the father. Thence going out and ascending to the summit of a hill overlooking his monastery, the Saint of God stood a little, and with uplifted hands blessed his community, and prophesied many things concerning the present and the future which the event afterwards confirmed.

CHAPTER XX.

When the Hour of Death is near, he makes a division of a Psalm.

AFTER these things, descending from the hill and being returned to the monastery, he was sitting in his cell writing a psalter. Coming at length to that verse of the thirty-third

Psalm, where it is written: "They that seek the Lord shall not want any good thing," he said : "Here I think I must stop. Baitheneus must write the words which follow." Now the verse which the Saint had just written applied very fitly to him to whom verily the good things of eternity will never be lacking. But to his successor, that is to the father of his spiritual sons, the following suited net less fitly ; "Come my children, hearken unto me, I will teach you the fear of the Lord." For, as his predecessor enjoined, he continued, not only in writing but also in labouring in the rule of the monastery.

CHAPTER XXI.

The Last Words of Columba.

ACCORDINGLY, after he had finished writing this verse, which completed the page, he went into the holy church to celebrate the Mass of the Lord's Day night. Returning to his dwelling as soon as it was ended, he sat all night on his bed, where for straw he was wont to have the bare floor, for a pillow a stone, which even to this day remains beside his sepulchre, as it were the inscription on his monument. So then sitting there he commended his last words to his children, saying : "Among yourselves have always mutual and unfeigned charity with peace ; but the Lord, the Comforter of the good, will be your aid, and I, abiding with Him, will intercede for you, that the good things of time and eternity may arise to you. After these words were said, S. Columba was silent for a little.

CHAPTER XXII.

Columba Dies in the Church.

THEN straightway at midnight, when the bell rang, rising hurriedly, he went to the church, and running more quickly than the rest, he entered alone, and fell down before the altar on bended knees in prayer. But Diormit, his servant, having followed more slowly, saw from afar at that moment the whole church filled from within with angelic light; as he drew near to the door the same light quickly vanished, but not before it had been seen by some of the brethren. But Diormit, entering the church, cried out repeatedly with tearful voice: "Where art thou, father?" And as lights had not yet been brought in by the brethren, he groped about in the darkness, and found the Saint lying upon his back before the altar. He raised him a little, and sitting beside him laid the holy head in his lap. But the other brethren running up and seeing that the father, whom they had loved while living, was dying, mourned exceedingly as he died. But the Saint, whose life had not yet passed away, raised his eyes to both sides, looked round with a joyful countenance, and saw the holy angels near. Diormit, having raised his right hand, signified that he should bless the brethren; but the holy father nodded to him and raised his hand himself as far as he could. And after his holy benediction thus signified, he straightway gave up the ghost. His face meanwhile remained ruddy, and in a wonderful degree enlivened by the angelic vision, so that it seemed to be the face not of the dead but of the sleeping.

CHAPTER XXIII.

His Burial.

MEANWHILE, after the departure of the holy soul, the hymns at Matins being finished, the sacred body was borne with the melodious singing of the brethren back from the church to his dwelling, where for three days and three nights his honourable obsequies were duly performed. When these were finished to the praise of God, the holy body, wrapped in clean linen cloths, was buried with due reverence, to be sometime raised in eternal glory.

CHAPTER XXIV.

A Storm occurs during the Days of his Obsequies as the Saint predicted.

FOR once one of the brethren said to the Saint : "All the people of the provinces will come after thy decease to thy obsequies." "No," said the Saint, "the event will not turn out as you say ; for a mixed crowd will not be present at my obsequies ; only my own monks with whom I have lived will fill my grave and honour my funeral with their attendance." And so it came to pass, for during those three days and nights of his obsequies, a great storm of wind without rain blew, so that no vessel was able to cross the sea to take part in the last rites of the man of God. At length, when the Saint was buried, the wind falling and the tempest being stilled, the waves of the sea became quiet. Glory to Thee O God. Amen.

CHAPTER XXV.

Eulogy of Columba. He raises the Dead. A Wonderful Stone. He Slays a Boar with a Word. He Blesses the Cows. He beholds souls received into Heaven. He appears to King Oswald. He predicts concerning King Aidan.

LET the reader therefore consider what and how great were the merits before God in the highest of him whom God so magnified by the prerogative of signs and the privilege of merits, and on whom, next to the Apostles, he bestowed the gift of his grace. For in the flesh, as an angel living, he stilled tempests, calmed seas, a Church not opened to him, he very often unlocked without a key, the bolt being uninjured, imprinting upon it only the sign of the Lord's cross. After kneeling some time, when he had poured himself out in prayer, rising from the ground, in the name of the Lord he brings to life the dead son of some common man, and after his obsequies are celebrated, he presents him alive to his father and mother. Also a stone dipped by him in water, in a wonderful way, contrary to its nature, floated upon the surface of the water, nor could this which the holy man had blessed be ever afterwards sunk. A sick man drank of the water in which it was swimming and immediately returned from the brink of death, and recovered soundness and health of body. Accordingly the same stone, afterwards preserved in the treasury of the King, wrought many cures among the people by the finger of God, by whom it had been blessed by the hand of Columba, the man of God. Again, when he has entered a wood, a boar of marvellous size, which the hounds chanced to be pursuing, meets him. At the sight of it the Saint stopped, and having raised his holy hand, said: "Come no further; die where thou art;" and it died. He also blessed five cows belonging to a poor man and commanded their number to increase to a hundred and five; and this rich blessing was upon the man's sons and grandsons. This Saint, too, very often beheld the souls of just men carried by angels into heaven, and those of wicked men taken down by demons to hell. Moreover, he spake to King Oswald, who had marked out his camp, in preparation for battle, and was sleeping in his tent on a cushion, and commanded him to go forth to battle. He obeyed the command and obtained the victory. Moreover, returning afterwards he was ordained by God Emperor of all Britain, and all the nation, who before that were unbelieving, were baptized. He likewise examined the whole world, clearly perceiving it as if collected under a single ray of the sun, its bosom being wonderfully opened to his merits. One day, also, the Saint of God instructed his servant to suddenly toll the bell. Aroused by the sound, the brethren forthwith entered the Church. The Saint said to them: "Pour out your prayers to the Lord for Aidan and his people." After a time he went out, and looking to heaven, said: "Now the barbarous host is turned to flight, and the victory is yielded to Aidan." Also in the spirit of prophecy he told them of the number of three hundred and three men of the army slain.

CHAPTER XXVI.

A Miracle Wrought by his Tunic.

AFTER the death of the man of God, a great drought occurred in the spring time. And the brethren fearing an approaching plague raised in the air the white tunic in which the blessed man was clad in the hour of death, and shook it thrice. They also read the books written by his own hand. When all these things were duly performed, wonderful to relate, on the same day a violent rain falling watered the thirsting land, and in the same year it produced rich crops.

CHAPTER XXVII.

AGAIN, once when the Saint was annoyed by a press of the brethren, a boy, very mean in countenance and dress, secretly drew near behind, that he might touch the fringe of the coat with which the Saint was clad without him knowing. But this was not hidden from the Saint ; for reaching his hand behind him, he held the boy's neck. To whom, trembling, the Saint said : "Open thy mouth and put out thy tongue ;" which doing, the Saint blessed him with outstretched hand, and said to those standing by : " This boy, now despicable to you, will from this hour be famous in all Ireland, and excel in wisdom, eloquence, in good manners, and in fruitfulness of virtues." Which, indeed, God fulfilled according to the prophecy of His Saint, to the praise and glory of His name, to whom is honour and glory for ever. Amen.

THE LIFE OF S. SERVANUS.

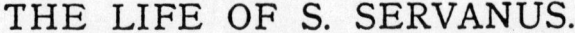

THE LIFE OF SERVANUS.

CHAPTER I.

THERE was a certain noble king in the land of Canaan by by name Obeth, the son of Eliud ; and the name of his wife was Alfia, the daughter of the King of Arabia. They lived together twenty years but had no offspring. Therefore they very frequently besought God and offered unto Him oblations and sacrifices that He would grant unto them a worthy child, in order that their reproach might be taken away. For this cause the King ordained through all His kingdom that all men from the least unto the greatest should fast three days and three nights and earnestly entreat the pity of God for the King and Queen, that the shame of sterility might be turned away from them. On the third night, at the last crowing of the cock, the angel of the Lord suddenly appeared to the King in a dream as he slept, saying : " Go to the city which is called Heliopolis and in it thou shalt find a very beautiful fountain and in it bathe three times. Afterwards you shall have what you desire." And departing, they came to the aforesaid fountain and did according to the saying of the angel. And the Queen desiring an herb growing by the fountain, which is called mandragon, she ate of it. After she had eaten thereof her husband went in unto her and she conceived. On the following night the angel appeared unto the Queen comforting her, and saying : " Be not sad nor sorrowful, O Queen ! for lo, thou bearest in thy womb two sons who shall excel in faith and works. The name of the one shall be Generatius ; that is, Shining Gem, and he shall be a great king over all the land of the Canaanites. The name of the other shall be Malachias or Servanus. And after he has finished the course of this secular life, these names will prove to have suited him well. For Malachias being interpreted is Angel of the Lord. This is a fit name for him, in that he lived as the ambassador of the Apostolic see, proclaiming the Word of God to the four quarters of the world. But he is called Servanus from serving God, in that he served our Lord Jesus Christ, labouring in every good work night and day." After saying these words the angel departed, and the Queen awoke and told her husband the words of the angel. Both therefore rejoiced and gave great thanks to God.

CHAPTER II.

AFTER the boy was born he was taken to the Bishop of the city of Alexandria, Mayonius by name, to be baptized by him. The Bishop baptized him and gave him the name Servanus. Blessed Servanus was accordingly nurtured seven years; and his father died. Now when his father was dead, they conferred upon him the government of the whole of their kingdom. But he, cleaving to God from his youth, opposed all their wishes; and his brother Generatius reigned in his stead. Now S. Servanus went to the city of Alexandria to devote himself there to divine study and to learn the arts. And there he remained thirteen years and received the habit of a monk from the bishop of that city. After thirty years, he was earnestly advised by the aforenamed Bishop that he ought to be promoted to sacred orders, inasmuch as he was deserving. Accordingly he was advanced to the order of the priesthood, though unwilling and gainsaying. Now after he was ordained he came into his own land, and all the Canaanites elected him with great joy to the bishopric. That bishopric he ruled in peace for twenty years, building monasteries and churches in it, and serving God day and night. Then the angel of the Lord came to him, saying: "Thou art commanded by the Lord God to go out and depart from thy country and from thy kindred." Blessed Servanus answered: "Freely will I go, but I know not whither my Lord desires me to go." The angel on this said to blessed Servanus : "I will be with thee whithersoever thou goest, delivering thee from every temptation of the devil ; and I will be thy companion, prospering the way of thy journey on sea and on land, from this day until the day of the dissolution of thy body." Then S. Servanus took leave of all the clerics and laity of his see and of his kindred and his friends, and blessed them. But they, lamenting his departure, earnestly besought him that he would not send them away desolate. But he, heeding not their tears and prayers, took his journey with a great multitude of companions, the angel guiding him.

CHAPTER III.

S. SERVANUS, afterwards, with fifty and ten thousand, came to the bank of the river Nile, and with all his company he safely crossed the river. Next, he arrived with them at the shore of the Red Sea, and they all crossed that sea with dry feet. Then after two months he came to the city of Jerusalem, and was there the honourable patriarch for seven years, in the place of James the Bishop, patriarch of the people of Jerusalem. Now, on a certain day the Angel said to S. Servanus ; "Ascend Mount Sion, and go round about it." S. Servanus ascended Mount Sion and went round about it. There was shown to him the tree from which the health-bringing Cross of Christ was hewn. Then the Angel said unto him :—"Cut from this tree four staves and carry them away with thee, and they shall be held in great virtue and reverence after you." At the voice of the Angel S. Servanus cut three staves. But the wood for a larger staff the Angel himself cut off and handed it to S. Servanus, and entrusted it to him. Thereafter the Saint held and preserved this staff in the greater honour and reverence. After these things he returned to Jerusalem with joy. And there the Angel said to him :—"It is time to leave this city and to go to the city of Constantinople, for this place is near to thy country and kindred." Blessed Servanus therefore arose and blessed all the inhabitants of Jerusalem, taking leave of them. After this he came to Constantinople with all the multitude of his companions, and was there honourably entertained for three years. Then being warned by the same Angel, he came to the land and to the island of Salvatoris. Now the island is called Salvatoris because in it our Saviour graciously came to us. Afterwards he came to Rome with a very great company. And the Romans learning his fame, which was noised abroad through all the countries and regions round about, received him with great honour. Now in these days the Romans were without a Pope and without a teacher. But the assembly of the clergy and people of Rome chose him to the Apostolate. And he was thus in the chair of Peter, ruling and teaching the Roman people, and doing signs and wonders seven years.

CHAPTER IV.

THE Angel of the Lord speaks with S. Servanus, saying, "Thy God commandeth thee to go out from this place, for it is too pleasant for thee to be here." Then Blessed Servanus addressed the Roman clergy and people, saying;—"Men, brethren, I take leave of you all and leave you all my benediction. For it behoves me, being warned of the Lord, to go into distant parts and to obey the Lord Jesus Christ in all things." On hearing this all the Romans were greatly displeased, for all the Roman people were of one mind to go with him, because they greatly loved a man so glorious in doctrine, manner and nobility. For they would rather endure hardness and privation in wandering through the world with him than be deprived of his presence and mellifluous doctrine. Nevertheless, he departed from the city of Rome with a great multitude of clergy and of the people, both men and women, sorrowing greatly over his departure, and came to the Hill of Tears. Blessed Servanus stood in this place, and turning to the people, said: " Men, brethren, and people beloved of God, grieve not over my departure nor be sorrowful, but divide yourselves into two companies; let one remain here at Rome; let the other lay aside all worldly care and follow me in this pilgrimage; for those who remain and for those who come with us I will pray God that He Himself may be with you, pardoning all your sins, and that He may have mercy upon us." All responded, " Amen." And the companies were separated and he blessed them with tears, and kissing them, said,—" Farewell, and abide in Christ."

CHAPTER V.

Now after Blessed Servanus with all his company ascends the Alps, he comes to the valley which is called Nigra, or the Valley of Beasts. And because Servanus knew that during that night he would be tempted of the devil, he passed the night in that valley. Then the angel said to the blessed man: " I make known to thee the pains which thou and all thine are about to suffer this night." And he said to him : " Comfort the crowds, and say to them that when the pains and torments of this night are passed, they will no more suffer the pains of hell." After this the angel departed, and S. Servanus came to the crowd, and comforting them, said : " Strengthen yourselves, and be ready to endure the pains which will this night come upon you." He set a verse before them as an example of prophecy, viz. : " Thou shalt tread on the asp, and the basilisk and the lion and the dragon shalt thou trample under foot." That is, You shall all, if you persevere in the faith of the Holy Trinity, tread on the asp and the basilisk, that is, on the devil and his pomps, and nothing shall harm you. Then the Saint said : " Eat and prepare yourselves for the coming wars." Now when they had finished eating and had repeated the verse, immediately there came a most black thick darkness over the valley in which they were. Then there came great earthquakes, thunders and lightnings, hail and sulphurous fires; and divers kinds of beasts, two-footed and four-footed, filled the valley round about them. Then came gnats having horny beaks, dragons, winged serpents, and every torment which the Prince of Darkness can show to man. When they saw all these things, great part of the crowd died. But S. Servanus, seeing that his companions were unable to endure these things, arose and blessed the valley, when all vanished and returned to nothing, and did no more hurt to any one. Then S. Servanus came with seven thousand thousands to the Ictean Sea which separates England from France, and they crossed it dry-shod. Thus God granted them a way and support on the sea. And afterwards he went from place to place until he came to the stream which is called the Forth. Now S. Edhennanus (Adamnan) was abbot in Scotland at that time, and he went to meet Servanus as far as the island of Keth (Inchkeith), and received him with great veneration because he had heard much good concerning him. When the space of one night was passed there, and after a time which it pleased them to enjoy in sweet conversation, S. Servanus said: "How shall I dispose of my household and companions?" S. Adamnan replied: "Let them dwell in the land of Fife and from the sea of the Britains as far as the mountain which is called Okhel." And so it was done.

CHAPTER VI.

AFTERWARDS S. Servanus, with only a hundred companions in his train, came to Kinel, and threw the branch which he held across the sea, and from it there grew an apple tree, which among the moderns is called Monglas. Then the Angel said to the blessed man: "There where that very beautiful tree has grown shall be the resting place of thy body." S. Servanus then came to the place which is called Culenros (Culross), desiring to dwell there, and cleared away all the thorns and thickets which abounded in the place. But the King of Scotia, namely, Brude, son of Dagart, who then held the kingdom of the Picts, was greatly enraged because without his permission he was dwelling there. Now the King sent his spearmen to slay S. Servanus with his whole household. Meanwhile a violent disease had attacked the King so that he had well nigh given up the ghost. He therefore hastily sent to the Saint of the Lord. The sick King spoke to the Saint as he came, saying : " O Saint of God, for the sake of Christ in whom thou believest, restore me to health and thou shalt have the place in which you dwell as a perpetual gift." The Saint, moved with the prayers and piety of the King, restored him to health. S. Servanus after this founded and dedicated a cemetery and his own Church in Culenros. The time there being fulfilled, he went to the island of Leven, that he might speak with S. Adamnan in person. Now S. Adamnan joyfully received the blessed man with honour, and thinking that he was seeking a place suitable for his religion, yielded that island to him as a gift with good will. Servanus therefore abode in it seven years, founded a monastery, and won many souls. Thence departing, he traversed and went round all the region of Fife, raising divers divine edifices to the Most High Creator.

CHAPTER VII.

On a certain occasion S. Servanus was in the cave at Dysart, and a certain brother, a monk, who was with him and was sick, desired a drink of wine and could not get one. Then Blessed Servanus took water from the fountain which is there and blessed it and changed the water into wine, and the sick man was healed. Moreover in that cave when S. Servanus was lying upon his couch after matins, the devil came to him, tempting him and disputing with him. And he said to him,

"Art thou a wise cleric, Servanus?" "What wishest thou O most miserable of all creatures?" The devil said: "I wish to dispute with thee and to question thee a little?" S. Servanus said: "Begin thou miserable wretch, begin." Satan asked him: "Where was God before He created the heavens and the earth, and before all the creatures were made?" Blessed Servanus said to him: "In Himself: for He is not local, and is held by no place, neither is He divided, nor subject to the motions of time, but is whole everywhere." And the devil said: "Why did God create creatures?" The Saint said: "Because there cannot be a Creator without creatures." "Wherefore did He make them very good?" To this the Saint replied: "Because God did not wish to do evil, or lest He should seem envious by being unwilling that aught should be good except Himself." The devil said: "Where did God form Adam?" The Saint said: "In Hebron." Satan said: "Where was he afterwards cast out from Paradise?" The Saint said: "Where he was formed." Satan said: "How long was he in Paradise after he had sinned?" The Saint replied: "Only seven hours." Satan said: "Why did God permit Adam and Eve to sin in Paradise?" To this the Saint replied: "Because God foresaw what great thing would come thereof. For Christ had not been born according to the flesh, had not Adam and Eve sinned." Satan said: "Why could not Adam and Eve be set free of themselves?" Servanus to this replied: "Because they did not fall of themselves, but through another, that is through the Devil persuading them. Therefore by another, that is Christ, born of their own stock they were set free." "Why did not God make a new man and send him to deliver the human race?" The Saint said: "Because he would not have pertained to us unless he had been of the race of Adam." "Why are you men delivered by the Passion of Christ, and not we demons?" "Because we have not the origin of our fall in ourselves, but from you demons? But as for you demons, because you are not of a fragile nature nor desire to repent and have contracted the origin of sin in yourselves, the Passion of Christ does not avail for you." The Devil therefore seeing that he could do nothing against the true Saint, and being vanquished in the interrogation, said : "Thou art wise Servanus, and I can dispute no more with thee." Servanus responded : "Go thou wretched creature, go and quickly depart hence, and never more venture to appear in this place to any man." And that place in honour of the holy, holy, holy Servanus, has been sacred up to this present day.

CHAPTER VIII.

MOREOVER, on a certain occasion blessed Servanus was at Tuligbotuan (Tillicoultry), and an evil spirit entered into a certain miserable man so that he had such a desire to eat, that he could in no wise be satisfied. S. Servanus placed his thumb in his mouth, and the devil crying out terribly came out of him and left him. On another occasion Blessed Servanus was in the same place, and a certain poor little woman brought forth two dead sons there, and bore them to blessed Servanus, and with tears besought him to restore them to life for her. But the Saint prostrated himself on the ground, and entreated our Lord God to look upon this woman, and in love to restore to her her offspring alive. Accordingly, God hearkened unto the prayer of the holy man, and restored to the mother both her children alive. On another night the same Saint was at Alva, being entertained by a certain poor peasant who had no substance, except one pig, which he killed that night for the holy man, and when he rose on the morrow, he found it alive in his yard. At another time there was a man in Aitheren who had a sheep which he loved and nourished in his house. But a thief coming stealthily stole it away from him. Now the ram was sought through the whole parish, and was not found, and lo! when the thief was brought into the presence of the blessed man and interrogated by the Saint whether he was guilty of the crime laid to his charge, he affirmed on oath that he was not. And beginning again to swear by the staff of the holy man, the wether bleated in his bowels. And the wretch confessed his sin, and asked and received pardon from S. Servanus.

At the time when the Saint was in the cell at Dunning, it was told him that a dragon great and terrible and very loathesome, whose look no mortal could endure, had come into his city. The Saint went out to meet it, and taking his staff in his right hand, fought with the dragon in a certain valley and slew it. From that day that valley is called the Dragon's Den. After these things there came to Blessed Servanus from the Alps three blind men and three lame men and three deaf men, who had been told that if they came to Blessed Servanus in Scotland, they would be healed, Therefore when they came they addressed the holy man, saluting him, and revealed to him the reason of their great labour and journey, and earnestly besought him to cure them of their infirmities. But the holy man, fearing that they said these things for the purpose of tempting him, spoke to them saying: "Men, brethren, think you I am God, or do you tempt me beyond what you see in me when you ask this great thing from me that I should heal you?" But they, prostrating themselves at his feet and bursting into tears, said with an oath: "No, lord father, no; but we believe that thy prayers and petitions avail much with God, and that we can obtain health through thee from the great Creator." Blessed Servanus, therefore, hearing their faith, blessed a certain fountain, and made them wash in it three times. And they, coming out thence, were made sound through the merit of the holy man. And thus the most holy Servanus gave sight to the blind, the power of walking to the lame, and hearing to the deaf. To these and to many others suffering divers kinds of diseases, he, through the power of God, gave and furnished health. Afterwards this Saint, beloved brethren, was assailed by a grievous infirmity, and was held down by the virulence of fever, and called all his brethren and announced to them that the day of his dissolution was near. Then the brethren wept much, and continuing instant in prayer to God for him, responded: "Why dost thou desert us, O Father? or to whom

wilt thou leave us desolate ones? For we would rather die
with thee than live in the world without thee." But the holy
man, after many miracles, after divers works, after founding
many churches in Christ, when he had bestowed peace on the
brethren, in the cell at Dunning, on the first day of the
Kalends of July, gradually yielded up his spirit and commended it to the Great Creator. After his death his disciples
and well nigh all the people of the whole province conveyed
his corpse to Culross. And there, with psalms and hymns and
chantings, they interred him honourably, where his merits and
the virtues of his merits flourish unto this day, to the praise
and honour of Almighty God, who in the perfect Trinity liveth
and reigneth for ever and ever. Amen.

THE LIFE OF S. MARGARET,

QUEEN OF SCOTLAND.

THE LIFE OF S. MARGARET.

PROLOGUE.

*To the honourable and excellent Matilda, Queen of the English,
T[urgot], a servant of the servants of S. Cuthbert, sends the
blessing of peace and health in this present life, and in the life
which is to come the blessing of all good things.*

FORASMUCH as you have requested, you have also commanded
me, to present to you in writing the story of the life of your
mother, whose memory is held in reverence, and of whose life,
which was well pleasing to God, you have often heard by the
concordant praise of many. You are wont to say that in this
matter my testimony is especially trustworthy, since you have
understood that by reason of her frequent and familiar intercourse with me I am acquainted with the most part of her
secrets. These your commands and desires I willingly obey ;
obeying them I greatly venerate them, and venerating them I
congratulate you, that, having been appointed by the King of
the Angels, Queen of the English, you desire not only to hear
about the life of the Queen, your mother, who ever longed for
the Kingdom of the Angels, but also to look upon it in writing
continually, so that, although you were but slightly acquainted
with her face, you may at least obtain a more perfect knowledge of her virtues. My own wish, indeed, is to fulfil your
commands, but I am wanting, I must own, in the ability ; the
materials for this undertaking being, in sooth, much greater
than I am able either by speech or writing to set forth.

2. Thus I am in a strait between two, and am drawn hither
and thither. On account of the greatness of the undertaking
I fear to obey ; and on account of the authority of you who

command, and the memory of her of whom I am to speak, I
dare not refuse. But, though I am unable to treat so great a
subject in the manner it deserves to be treated, I am nevertheless bound, as far as in me lies, to make it known. I owe this
to the love I have for her and to the obedience which is due to
your command. The grace of the Holy Spirit, which gave
such efficacy to her virtues, will vouchsafe help to me, I trust,
to narrate them. " The Lord shall give the word to them that
preach good tidings with great power," and again, " Open thy
mouth wide and I will fill it." For no man can fail in the
Word who believes in the Word. " In the beginning was the
Word, and the Word was God." In the first place, therefore,
I desire that you, and that through you others, should know
that if I were to attempt to relate all that could be told respect-
ing her, I should be thought to be flattering you under cover of
your mother's praises on account of the greatness of your
queenly dignity. But far be it from my grey hairs to mingle
the crime of falsehood with the virtues of such a woman, in
setting forth which, I profess, God is my Witness and Judge,
that I add nothing to the truth; but suppress many things
lest they should seem incredible, and that I may not be said,
as the orator has it, to be decking out a crow with the colours
of a swan.

CHAPTER I.

Her noble descent and virtues as a Queen and as a Mother.

MANY, as we read, have derived the origin of their name from
a quality of the mind, so that there is shewn in respect to
them a correspondence between the word of their name and
the grace they have received. Thus Peter was so named from
" the Rock," that is Christ, on account of the firmness of his
faith ; so John, that is " the grace of God," because of his con-
templation of the Divinity and his prerogative of the Divine
love ; and the sons of Zebedee were called Boanerges, that is,

the Sons of Thunder, because they thundered forth the preaching of the Gospel. The same was true of this virtuous woman,
in whom the fairness indicated by her name was surpassed by
the exceeding beauty of her soul. She was called Margaret,
i.e. a Pearl, and in the sight of God she was esteemed a goodly
pearl by reason of her faith and good works. She was a pearl
indeed to you, to me, to us all, yea even to Christ; and because she was Christ's, she is all the more ours, now that she
has left us and is taken to the Lord. This pearl I say was
taken from the dunghill of this world and now shines in her
place among the jewels of the Eternal King. This I think no
one will doubt, when he has read the following account of her
life and death. When I recall the conversations I had with her,
seasoned as they were with the salt of wisdom, when I think
of the tears wrung from her by the compunction of her heart,
when I consider the sobriety and staidness of her manners and
remember her affability and prudence, I rejoice while I lament,
and while lamenting I rejoice. I rejoice, because she has
passed away to God after whom she longed; I lament, because I am not rejoicing with her in the heavenly places. I
rejoice for her, I say, because she now sees in the land of the
living the goodness of the Lord in which she believed; but for
myself I mourn, because as long as I suffer the miseries of this
mortal life in the land of the dead, I am daily compelled to
cry, " O wretched man that I am, who shall deliver me from
the body of this death ?"

4. Since, then, I am to speak of that nobility of mind which
she had in Christ, it is fitting that something should be first
said of that nobility by which she was also distinguished
according to this world. Her grandfather was King Edmund,
who, because he was strong in battle and invincible by his
enemies, derived his distinctive name from the excellence of
his valour, for he was called in English Ironsides. His brother
on his father's side, but not on his mother's, was the most
religious and meek Edward, who proved himself the Father of
his Country; and as another Solomon, that is, a lover of peace,
protected his kingdom by peace rather than by arms. He had
a mind that subdued anger, despised avarice, and was entirely

free from pride. And no wonder; for as he derived the glory of his kingly rank from his ancestors, so also he derived from them, as by hereditary right, the nobility of his life; being descended from Edgar, King of the English, and from Richard, Count of the Normans, his grandfathers on either side, men who were not only most illustrious, but also most religious. Of Edgar, in order to describe how great he was in this world and what he was in Christ, it may be briefly said that he was marked out beforehand both as a King and as a lover of justice and peace. For at his birth S. Dunstan heard the holy angels rejoicing in heaven and singing with great joy: "Let there be peace, let there be joy in the Church of the English, as long as this new-born boy shall hold the kingdom and Dunstan runs the course of this mortal life."

5. Richard, also, the father of Emma, the mother of this Edward, was an illustrious ancestor worthy of so noble a grandchild. He was a man of the greatest energy, and deserving of every praise. None of his forefathers ruled the earldom of Normandy with greater prosperity and honour, or were more fervent in their love of religion. Endowed with great riches, like a second David, he was poor in spirit; exalted to be lord over his people, he was a lowly servant of the servants of Christ. Among other things which he did as memorials of his love of religion, this devout worshipper of Christ built that noble monastery of Fecamp, in which he was often wont to reside with the monks, and where, in the habit of a secular but in heart a monk, he used to place the food of the brethren on the table when they were eating their silent meal, and serve them with drink; so that, according to the Scripture, " The greater he was the more he humbled himself in all things." If any one wishes to know more fully his works of magnificence and virtue, let him read the *Acts of the Normans*, which contains his history. From ancestors so renowned and illustrious, Edward, their grandchild, did in no wise degenerate. On the father's side only, as was before said, he was the brother of King Edmund, from whose son came Margaret, who by the splendour of her merits completes the glory of this illustrious family.

6. While therefore Margaret was still in the flower of her youth, she began to lead a life of great strictness, to love God above all things, to occupy herself with the study of the Holy Scriptures, and to exercise her mind therein with joy. Keen penetration of intellect was hers to understand any matter whatever it might be, tenacity of memory to retain many things, and a graceful facility of language to give expression to her thoughts. While therefore she meditated in the law of the Lord day and night, and, like another Mary, sitting at His feet, she delighted to hear His word, by the desire of her friends rather than by her own, yea, rather by the appointment of God, she was married to Malcolm, son of Duncan, the most powerful King of the Scots. But though compelled to do the things which are of the world, she deemed it beneath her to set her affections upon them ; for she delighted more in good works than in abundance of riches. With things temporal she procured for herself everlasting rewards ; for in heaven where her treasure was, there she had placed her heart. And because before all things she sought the kingdom of God and His righteousness, the abundant grace of the Almighty freely added to her honours and riches. All things which became the rule of a prudent Queen were done by her ; by her advice the laws of the kingdom were administered ; by her zeal the true religion was spread and the people rejoiced in the prosperity of their affairs. Nothing was more firm than her faith, more constant than her favour, more enduring than her patience, weightier than her counsel, more just than her decisions, or more pleasant than her conversation.

7. After she had attained this high dignity, she at once, in the place where her nuptials were celebrated, built an eternal monument of her name and devotion. For she erected the noble church there in honour of the Holy Trinity with a threefold purpose ; for the redemption of the King's soul, for the good of her own, and to obtain prosperity in this life and in the life that is to come for her children. This church she adorned with divers kinds of precious gifts, among which, as is well known, were vessels not a few of solid and pure gold for the holy service of the altar, of which I can speak with the

greater certainty, since by the Queen's commands, I myself
for a long time had them all under my charge there. A cross,
also, of incomparable value, having upon it an image of the
Saviour which she had caused to be covered with a vestment
of purest gold and silver studded with gems, she placed there,
which proves to those who behold it even now the earnestness
of her faith. To this the Church of St. Andrews bears witness,
where is preserved, as is seen to this day, a most beautiful
crucifix which she erected there. Without these things, those,
I mean, which belong to the celebration of the divine service,
her chamber was never found ; it seemed, so to say, to be the
workshop of a heavenly artificer. There were always to be
seen in it copes for the cantors, chasubles, stoles, altar-cloths,
also other priestly vestments and church ornaments. Some
were in course of preparation, others, already finished, were of
admirable beauty.

8. With these works women of noble birth and approved
gravity of conduct who were deemed worthy to be engaged in
the Queen's service, were entrusted. No men were admitted
among them, save such as she allowed to accompany her when
she sometimes paid them a visit. There was no unseemly
familiarity among them with the men, nor any pert frivolity.
For the Queen united such strictness to her sweetness and
such sweetness to her strictness that all who were in her service, men as well as women, while fearing loved her and while
loving feared her. Wherefore in her presence no one ventured
to do anything wrong, or even to utter an unseemly word.
For repressing all evil in herself, there was great gravity in her
joy and something noble in her anger. Her mirth was never
expressed in immoderate laughter ; when angry she never
gave way to fury. Always angry with her own faults, she
sometimes reproved those of others with that commendable
anger tempered with justice which the Psalmist enjoined, when
he says : " Be angry and sin not." Her whole life, regulated
with the utmost skill of discretion, was, as it were, a pattern of
the virtues. Her conversation was seasoned with the salt of
wisdom : her silence was filled with good thoughts. Her
bearing so corresponded with the gravity of her character that

she might be believed to have been born simply to show what comeliness of life is. But to speak briefly, in whatever she was wont to say or do, she showed that her mind was dwelling on things divine.

9. Nor did she spend less pains upon her children than upon herself, that they might be brought up with the utmost care, and especially that they might be trained in virtue. Hence because she knew the Scripture: He that spareth the rod hateth his child, she instructed the governor of the nursery as often as the children fell into such faults as are common to their age, to curb them with threats and the rod. By reason of their mother's religious care they excelled many who were of greater age in their good behaviour. Among themselves they were always kindly and peaceable, and the younger everywhere paid respect to the elder. Hence, also, during the celebration of the Mass, when they went up after their parents to make their offerings, the younger never in any way presumed to precede the older, but the older were wont to go before the younger according to their age. She would often call them to her, and, as far as their age would allow, instruct them concerning Christ and the faith of Christ, and carefully endeavour to admonish them to always fear Him. "O my children," she would say, "fear the Lord; for they that fear Him shall not want anything that is good; and if you love Him, He will give you, my darlings, prosperity in this life and eternal felicity with all the saints." This was the mother's desire, her admonition, the prayer which she uttered day and night with tears for her little ones, that they might acknowledge their Maker in the faith that worketh by love, and acknowledging worship Him, and worshipping Him, love Him in all things and above all things, and loving Him attain to the glory of the heavenly kingdom.

CHAPTER II.

Her care for the honour of the Kingdom and discipline of the Church.
Abuses corrected.

NOR need we wonder that the Queen ruled herself and her household wisely, since she was always guided by the most wise counsel of the Holy Scriptures. For what I used frequently to admire in her was that amid the distraction of law-suits, and the countless affairs of the Kingdom, she gave herself with wonderful diligence to the reading of the Word of God, concerning which she used to ask profound questions of the learned men who were sitting near her. But as among them no one had a profounder intellect, so no one had the power of clearer expression. Thus it often happened that these teachers left her much more learned than when they came. She had a religious and earnest desire for the sacred volumes, and very often her affectionate familiarity with me urged me to exert myself to obtain them for her. Nor in these things was she anxious for her own salvation alone; she sought also that of others. And first of all, with the help of God, she made the King himself most attentive to works of justice, mercy, alms-giving, and other virtues. From her also he learned to keep the vigils of the night in prayer: from her exhortation and example he learned to pray with groanings from the heart and abundance of tears. I confess I marvelled at this great miracle of the mercy of God when I saw such earnestness of devotion in the King, and such sorrow in the heart of a layman when engaged in prayer.

11. A Queen whose life was so venerable, he as it were feared to offend, since he clearly perceived that Christ was truly dwelling in her heart; he hastened rather the more quickly to obey in all things her wishes and prudent counsels. What she refused he refused, and what she loved, he loved for the love of her love. Hence also the books which she used either in her devotions or for reading, he, though unable to read, used often to handle and examine, and when he heard

from her that one of them was dearer to her than the others,
this he also regarded with kindlier affection, and would kiss
and often fondle it. Sometimes also he would send for the
goldsmith, and instruct him to adorn the volume with gold and
precious stones, and when finished he would carry it to the
Queen as a proof of his devotion. The Queen, on the other
hand, herself the noblest gem of a royal race, made the
splendour of her husband's royal magnificence much more
splendid, and contributed much glory and honour to all the
nobility of the kingdom and their retainers. For she brought
it to pass that merchants who came by land and sea from
divers lands, brought with them for sale many and precious
kinds of merchandise which in Scotland were before unknown,
among which, at the instigation of the Queen, the people
bought garments of various colours, and different kinds of
personal ornaments ; so that from that time they went about
clothed in new costumes of different fashions, from the elegance
of which they might have been supposed to be a new race.
She also appointed a higher class of servants for the King,
that when he walked or rode abroad numerous bodies of them
might accompany him in state ; and this was carried out with
such discipline that wherever they came none of them was
permitted to take anything from anyone by force ; nor did any
of them dare to oppress or injure the country people or the
poor in any way. Moreover, she increased the splendour of the
royal palace, so that not only was it brightened by the different
coloured uniforms worn in it, but the whole house was made
resplendent with gold and silver ; for the vessels in which the
King and nobles of the kingdom were served with food and
drink, were either of gold or silver, or with gold or silver
plated.

12. And this the Queen did not because the honour of the
world delighted her, but because she felt compelled to do what
the royal dignity required of her. For when she walked in
state clad in splendid apparel, as became a Queen, like another
Esther, she in her heart trod all these trappings beneath her
feet, and bore in mind that under the gems and gold there was
nothing but dust and ashes. In a word, in the midst of her

exalted dignity she always took the greatest care to preserve her lowliness of mind. It was easy for her to repress all swellings of pride arising from worldly glory, inasmuch as the fleeting nature of this frail life never escaped from her thoughts. For she always remembered the text in which the miserable condition of human life is described: "Man that is born of woman, is of few days, and full of trouble. He cometh forth like a flower, and is cut down, and fleeth also as a shadow and continueth not." She meditated continually also on that passage of the Blessed Apostle James, in which he says: "What is your life? It is even a vapour that appeareth for a little time, and then vanisheth away." And because as the Scripture says, "Happy is the man that feareth alway," this venerable Queen made it the easier for her to avoid sin, as in fear and trembling she continually kept before her mind's eye the dreadful day of Judgment. Hence she frequently entreated me not to hesitate to point out and reprove in private anything which I saw amiss in her words or actions. Because I did this less frequently and sharply than she wished, she urged the duty on me and accused me of being asleep and, as it were, negligent towards her: "The just man," she said, "shall correct me in mercy, and shall reprove me; but let not the oil of the sinner, that is the flattery, fatten my head;" for "Better are the wounds of a friend than the deceitful kisses of an enemy." She would say this because she sought censure as helping her advancement in virtue, where another might have regarded it as a disgrace.

13. This religious and devout Queen, while she thus in mind and word and deed journeyed on to the heavenly country, also invited others to accompany her on the undefiled way, in order that they with her might attain true happiness. The wicked whom she saw, she admonished to become good; the good to be better, and the better to strive to be best. The zeal of God's house, which is the Church, consumed her so that, aglow with Apostolic faith, she laboured to root out entirely those unlawful things which had sprung up within it. For when she saw that many things were done among the Scottish people which were contrary to the rule of the right faith and the holy

custom of the universal Church, she appointed frequent councils to be held, in order that by some means or other she might, through the gift of Christ, bring back the wandering into the way of truth. Of these councils, the most important is that in which she alone, with a very few of her friends, for three days combatted the defenders of a perverse custom with the sword of the Spirit, that is, with the Word of God. You would have thought that another Helena was present; for just as she formerly overcame the Jews with the authority of the Scriptures, so now did this Queen those who were in error. At their discussion the King himself was present as an assessor and chief actor, fully prepared to say and do whatever she in this matter might direct. And as he knew the English language quite as well as his own, he was in this Council a most expert watchful interpreter for either side.

14. The Queen opened the proceedings by remarking that all who serve one God in one faith along with the Catholic Church ought not to vary from that Church by new or strange usages. She then pointed out in the first place that they were observing the fast of Lent in a way which was not lawful, inasmuch as they were in the habit of beginning it not with the Holy Catholic Church on the fourth day of the week at the beginning of Lent, but on the Monday of the week following. To this they answered : "The fast which we observe, we keep according to the authority of the Gospel, which states that Christ fasted six weeks." She replied by saying: "In this matter you differ widely from the Gospel, for we read there that the Lord fasted forty days, which you clearly do not do. For when during the six weeks, six Lord's days are deducted from the fast, it is plain that only thirty and six days remain for fasting. Plainly therefore the fast which you keep is not the forty days enjoined by the Gospel, but one of thirty and six days. It remains therefore for you, if you wish to observe an abstinence of forty days, after our Lord's example, to begin to fast with us four days before Quadragesima ; otherwise you alone will be acting contrary to the authority of our Lord, and in opposition to the tradition of the entire Holy Church." Convinced by this clear demonstration of the truth, they

henceforth began the solemnities of the sacred fasts at the same
time as Holy Church does everywhere.

15. The Queen also raised another point, and required them
to explain for what reason they neglected to receive the
Sacrament of the Body and Blood of Christ at Easter according to the custom of the Holy and Apostolic Church. They
answered : " The Apostle speaking of those who celebrate the
Lord's Supper says : ' He that eateth and drinketh unworthily,
eateth and drinketh judgment to himself.' And hence because
we acknowledge that we are sinners, we fear to approach that
mystery lest we should eat and drink judgment to ourselves."
" What ! " said the Queen, " Shall all who are sinners not taste
that holy mystery ? No one therefore ought to receive it, for
there is not one who is not stained with sin ; not even the
infant whose life is but one day on the earth. And if no one
ought to receive it, why did the Lord when he proclaimed the
Gospel say, ' Except ye shall eat the flesh of the Son of Man,
and drink His blood, ye shall not have life in you.' But if you
would understand the passage you have adduced from the
Apostle in the same way as the Father, it is evident that you
must take quite another view of it. For the Apostle does not
say that all sinners are unworthy to receive the sacraments of
salvation, for after saying, ' he eateth and drinketh judgment
to himself,' he adds, ' Not discerning the Body of our Lord,'
that is, not distinguishing it in faith from bodily foods, ' he
eateth and drinketh judgment to himself.' But he who without
confession and penance, and with the defilement of his sins
presumes to draw near to the sacred mysteries—he it is, I say,
who eats and drinks judgment to himself. But we who many
days previously have made confession of our faults, are
chastened with penance and fasts, and washed from the stains
of our sins by almsgiving and tears—we on the day of the
resurrection of the Lord, approaching His Table in the Catholic
Faith, receive the Body and Blood of the Immaculate Lamb,
Jesus Christ, not to judgment, but to the remission of sins and
to the salutary preparation of our souls for the reception of
eternal blessedness." To these arguments they could make no

reply, and understanding now the practices of the Church, observed them in the reception of the mystery of salvation.

16. Moreover, there were some in certain parts of Scotland who were wont to celebrate Masses according to I know not what barbarous rite, contrary to the custom of the whole Church. This the Queen, fired by zeal for God, sought to destroy and abolish, so that henceforth throughout the whole of Scotland there was no one who presumed to continue any such practice. It was their custom also to neglect the reverence due to the Lord's Day, and to follow their earthly occupation on that day as on others—a practice she showed them which was forbidden both by reason and authority. "Let us reverence the Lord's Day," she said, "because of the Lord's Resurrection, which took place upon it; let us no longer do servile works on the day on which we know that we were redeemed from the bondage of the devil. This also the Blessed Pope Gregory affirms, saying: 'On the Lord's Day we ought to abstain from earthly labour, and devote ourselves wholly to prayer, in order that if during the six days we have been negligent in anything, we may on the Lord's Day expiate it by prayers.' The same Father, Gregory, after condemning one with the greatest warmth for a certain piece of earthly work which he had done on the Lord's Day, decreed that those on whose advice he had done it should be excommunicated for two months." Unable to contradict these arguments of the wise Queen, they henceforward at her instance observed the Lord's Days with such reverence that no one dared to carry a burden on them, nor did any man venture to compel another to do so. Next she showed how utterly abominable, and to be shunned by the faithful as death itself, was the unlawful marriage of a man with his step-mother, or with the widow of his deceased brother; both of which customs had hitherto prevailed in the country. Many other abuses also which had grown up contrary to the rule of faith and the institutions and observances of the Church, she likewise in this Council succeeded in condemning and expelling from the Kingdom. For whatever she proposed, she so supported with the testimony of the Holy Scriptures and with citations from the holy Fathers, that no one on the

opposite side could say anything at all against it ; nay, rather, laying aside their obstinacy and yielding to reason, they willingly undertook to adopt whatever she desired.

CHAPTER III.

Her charity towards the poor.   Her manner of passing Lent.   Her prayerfulness.

THUS the venerable Queen, who by the help of God had endeavoured to cleanse His house from defilements and errors, was found day by day as the Holy Spirit illuminated her heart, more and more meet to become His temple.   And such I well know she truly was, for I both saw the works which she did outwardly, and knew her conscience, for she revealed it to me.   She condescended to converse with me in the most familiar way, and to disclose to me her secret thoughts ; not because there was anything good in me, but because she thought there was.   When she conversed with me concerning the salvation of the soul and the sweetness of the life which is eternal, she uttered words so full of all grace that the Holy Spirit, which truly dwelt in her heart, evidently spoke by her lips.   And so deeply was she moved while speaking, that it might have been thought that she would be wholly dissolved in tears, and at her compunction I also was moved to weeping. Beyond all whom I have ever known she devoted herself to prayer and fasting, and to works of mercy and almsgiving. Let me speak first of her prayerfulness.   In a church no one was ever more silent or composed, and in prayer no one was ever more earnest.   For while in the house of God she would never speak of worldly matters, nor do anything which savoured of the earth.   It was her custom there only to pray, in prayer to pour forth her tears.   In the body only was she here on earth ; her soul was with God ; for besides God and the things which are God's, in her pure supplications she sought nothing.

But what shall I say of her fasting? This only, that by her
too great abstinence she brought upon herself a very serious
infirmity.

18. To these two, that is, to prayer and fasting, she joined
the gifts of mercy. For what could be more compassionate
than her heart? What more gentle to the needy? Not only
would she give her goods to the poor, but if she could, she
would have freely given herself. She was poorer than any of
her paupers, for they, having nothing, desired to have, but she
was anxious to dispose what she had. When she walked or
rode out in public, crowds of poor people, orphans and widows,
flocked to her as they would to a most beloved mother, and
none of them ever left her without being comforted. And
when all she had brought with her for the use of the needy had
been distributed, she used to receive from her attendants and
the rich who accompanied her their garments and anything
else they had with them at the time, to bestow upon the poor,
so that no one might ever go away from her in distress. Nor
did those who were with her take this ill; they rather strove
among themselves to offer her what they had, since they knew
for certain that she would pay them the double of what they
had given. Now and then she took something or other, whatever it might be, from the King's private property to give to a
poor person, and the King always took this pious plundering
in good part and pleasantly. On Maundy Thursday and at
High Mass he used to make an offering of gold coins, and
some of these she would often piously steal and give away to
the beggar who was importuning her for alms. Often indeed
the King, who was quite aware of what she was doing, though
he pretended not to know anything about it, was greatly
amused at this kind of theft, and sometimes, when he caught
her in the act with the coins in her hand, would jocularly
threaten to have her arrested, tried, and condemned. Nor was
it to the poor of her own people alone that she exhibited the
abundance of her cheerful and open-handed charity, those also
were sharers of her bounty whom the fame of her liberality
drew towards her from almost every other nation. Of a truth,

to her may be applied the Scripture: "He hath dispersed; he hath given to the poor; his righteousness endureth for ever."

19. But who can tell the number of the English of all ranks carried away captive from their own country by the violence of war, and reduced to slavery, whom she restored to liberty by paying their ransom? She sent secret spies everywhere throughout the provinces of Scotland to ascertain who among the captives were oppressed with the more cruel bondage or were the more inhumanely treated, and to report privately to her where they were and by whom they were ill-treated; and, commiserating them from the bottom of her heart, she hastened to their assistance, paid their ransom, and restored them to freedom. At that time there were very many in different parts of the kingdom of Scotland who, shut up in separate cells, were leading lives of great strictness, in the flesh but not according to the flesh, for though on this earth, they were living the life of angels. In these the Queen venerated Christ and loved Him, and frequently occupied herself in visiting and conversing with them, and used to commend herself to their prayers. And since she could not prevail upon them to accept from her any earthly gift, she used to earnestly entreat them to honour her by prescribing for her some work of almsgiving or mercy; and forthwith this devout woman did whatever they desired, either by rescuing the poor out of their poverty or by relieving the afflicted from the miseries by which they were oppressed.

20. Since the church of St. Andrews was much frequented by the devout, who flocked to it from all sides, she erected dwellings on either shore of the sea which divides Lothian from Scotland, that, after the fatigues of their journey, pilgrims and the poor might take shelter and rest, and there find already prepared for them all they needed for the refreshment of the body; for she had appointed servants whose exclusive duty was always to have in readiness everything that these wayfarers might need, and to attend to them with the greatest care. She also provided ships for the transport of these pilgrims, both coming and going; nor was any toll ever levied from those who were ferried across.

21. As I have spoken of the daily manner of life of this

venerable Queen, and of her daily works of mercy, I will now attempt to give a brief account of how she used to spend the forty days before Christmas and the whole season of Lent. After she had rested a little at the beginning of the night, she went into the church, and there alone she completed first the Matins of the Holy Trinity, next the Matins of the Holy Cross, and then the Matins of Our Lady. When these were ended she began the Offices of the Dead, and after these the Psalter, nor did she cease until she had gone through it. While the priests were saying the Matins and Lauds at the fitting hour, she either finished the Psalter she had begun, or if she had finished it, began it a second time. When she had gone through the office of the Matins and Lauds, she returned to her chamber, and along with the King himself washed the feet of six poor persons, and used to give them something wherewith they might relieve their poverty. It was the Chamberlain's especial duty to bring these poor people in every night before the Queen's arrival, so that she might find them ready when she came to wait upon them. After she had waited upon them, she betook herself to rest and sleep.

22. When the day dawned she rose from bed, and continued for a long time in prayer and reading the Psalms, and whilst reading them performed this work of mercy—nine orphan little children, who were utterly destitute, she caused to be brought in to her at the first hour of the day in order that she might feed them. For she ordered soft food, such as little children delight in, to be prepared for them daily ; and when the little ones were brought to her, she did not think it beneath her to take them on her knee and make little sups for them, and to place them in their mouths with the spoons she herself used. Thus the Queen, who was honoured by all the people, performed for Christ's sake the office of a most devoted servant and mother. To her the words of the Blessed Job might very fittingly be applied : " From my infancy mercy grew up with me, and it came out with me from my mother's womb." While this was going on, it was the custom to bring three hundred poor people into the royal hall, and when they had been seated round it in order, the King and Queen came in, and the doors

were shut by the servants, for with the exception of the chaplains, certain religious, and a few attendants, no one was permitted to witness their alms-givings. The King on the one side, and the Queen on the other, waited upon Christ in the person of His poor, and with great devotion served them with food and drink, which had been specially prepared for this purpose. When this was finished, the Queen used to go into the Church and there offer herself a sacrifice to God with many prayers, sighs, and tears. For besides the Hours of the Holy Trinity, the Holy Cross, and the Holy Mary, recited within the space of a day and a night, she would on these holy days repeat the Psalter twice or thrice, and before the celebration of the Public Mass cause five or six Masses to be sung privately in her presence.

23. By the time these things were finished, the time for eating was at hand, but before taking her own food she fed twenty-four poor people, whom she humbly waited upon herself. For besides the many alms-deeds I have spoken of already, she supported poor people to this number, that is, twenty-four, throughout the whole course of the year as long as she lived. These she desired to live near to wherever she herself was living, and to accompany her wherever she went. After she had devoutly waited upon Christ in these, she used to refresh her own feeble body. In this meal, since according to the Apostle we ought not to make provision for the lust of the flesh, she hardly allowed herself the necessaries of life, for she ate only to sustain life and not to please her palate. Her light and frugal meal excited rather than satisfied her hunger. She seemed to taste her food, not to take it. From this let it be considered, I beseech you, how great her abstinence was when she fasted, when such was her abstinence when she feasted. And though her whole life was one of great temperance, yet during these fasts, that is, during the forty days preceding Easter and Christmas, the abstinence with which she was in the habit of afflicting herself was incredible. Hence, on account of her excessive fasting, she suffered up to the end of her life from a very acute pain in the stomach. Nevertheless, her bodily infirmity did not impair

her virtue in good works. Assiduous in reading the sacred Scriptures, instant in prayer, and unceasing in alms-giving, she exercised herself continually and watchfully in all things pertaining to God. And because she knew the Scripture: "Whom the Lord loveth, he chasteneth, and scourgeth every son whom he receiveth," she accepted the pains of her body willingly, and with patience and thanksgiving, as the stripes of a most gracious Father.

24. Since therefore she was devoted to these and similar works, and struggled with her continual infirmities, God's strength, to use the words of the Apostle, was made perfect in her weakness, and going on from strength to strength, she was each day made better. Forsaking in her heart all earthly things, she longed with her whole soul for the things of heaven, yea, thirsted for them, crying out with her heart and voice with the Psalmist: "My soul thirsteth for God, for the living God; when shall I come and appear before God." Let others admire the tokens of miracles which they see in others, I, for my part, admire much more the works of mercy which I saw in Margaret. Miracles are common to the evil and to the good, but the works of true piety and charity belong to the good alone. The former sometimes indicate holiness, but the latter are holiness itself. Let us, I say, admire in Margaret the things which made her a saint, rather than the miracles, if she did any, which might only have indicated that she was one to men. Let us more worthily admire her as one in whom, because of her devotion to justice, piety, mercy, and love, we see rather the works of the ancient Fathers than their miracles. Nevertheless, it will not be out of place if I here narrate one incident which seems to me to indicate the holiness of her life.

25. She had a book of the Gospels beautifully adorned with jewels and gold, and ornamented with the figures of the four Evangelists, painted and gilt. The capital letters throughout the volume were also resplendent with gold. For this volume she had always a greater affection than she had for any others she was in the habit of reading. It happened that while the person who was carrying it was crossing a ford, he let the vol-

ume, which had been carelessly folded in a wrapper, fall into
the middle of the stream, and, ignorant of what had occurred,
he quietly continued his journey. But when he afterwards
wished to produce the book, he, for the first time, became
aware that he had lost it. It was sought for for a long time,
but was not found. At length it was found at the bottom of
the river, lying open, so that its leaves were kept in constant
motion by the action of the water, and the little coverings of
silk which protected the letters of gold from being injured by
the contact of the leaves, were carried away by the force of the
current. Who would imagine that the book would be worth
anything after what had happened to it? Who would believe
that even a single letter would have been visible in it? Yet of
a truth it was taken up out of the middle of the river so perfect, uninjured, and free from damage, that it looked as though
it had not even been touched by the water. For the whiteness
of the leaves, and the form of the letters throughout the whole
of the volume remained exactly as they were before it fell into
the river, except that on the margin of the leaves, towards the
edge, some trace of the water could with difficulty be detected.
The book was conveyed to the Queen, and the miracle reported
to her at the same time, and she having given thanks to Christ,
esteemed the volume much more highly than she did before.
Wherefore let others consider what they should think of this,
but as for me I am of opinion that this miracle was wrought
by our Lord because of His love for this venerable Queen.

CHAPTER IV.

The Queen's preparations for her end. Her sickness and happy death.

MEANTIME, while Almighty God was preparing everlasting
rewards for her works of devotion, she was preparing herself,
with more than her usual carefulness, for entering another life.
For, as her own word a little after showed, it would appear that
her own departure from this life and certain other events were

known to her long before they occurred. Therefore summoning me to come to her privately, she began to recount to me in order the story of her life, and as she proceeded shed floods of tears. In short, so great was her compunction while she conversed with me, and out of her compunction there sprang such an abundance of tears, that, as it seemed to me, there was, beyond all doubt, nothing which she might not at that time have obtained from Christ. As she wept I also wept; thus for a time we wept and at times were silent, since by reason of our sobs we were unable to give utterance to our words. The flame, as it were, of the compunction which consumed her heart reached my own soul also, borne into it by the spiritual fervour of her words. And when I heard the words of the Holy Ghost speaking by her tongue and clearly perceived her conscience revealed by her words, I judged myself unworthy of the grace of so great a familiarity.

27. When she had ceased to speak of the things which it was needful for her to speak, she began to address me again, saying : " Farewell, I shall not remain long with you in this life ; but you will survive me for a considerable time. Two things, therefore, I beg of you. One is, that as long as you live you will remember me in your prayers and at the Mass; the other is, that you will take some care of my sons and daughters, pour out your affection upon them, above all things teach them to fear and love God, and never cease from instructing them ; and when you see any of them exalted to the height of earthly dignity, then at once, as a father or a teacher in the highest sense, go to him, warn, and when circumstances require it, censure him, lest, on account of a passing honour, he be puffed up with pride, or offend God with avarice, or through the prosperity of the world neglect the blessedness of life eternal. These are the things," she said, "which I ask you, as in the sight of God who is now present along with us two, to promise me that you will carefully do." At these words I again burst into tears and promised her that I would carefully perform what she had asked me ; for I did not dare to oppose one whom I heard unhesitatingly predict what was to come to pass. The truth of her prediction has now been verified by the things

which now are ; since I live and she is dead and I see her offspring raised to dignity and honour. Thus having finished
her conference with me and being about to return home I said
farewell to the Queen for the last time ; for I saw her face no
more.

28. Not long after this she was attacked by an illness more
severe than usual, and was purified by the fire of a tedious
sickness before the day on which she was called away. I will
describe her death as I heard it narrated by her priest, whom,
on account of his simplicity, innocence, and purity, she loved
more intimately than the others, and who after her death gave
himself to Christ in perpetual service for her soul, and having
put on the monk's habit, offered himself as a sacrifice for her
at the tomb of the incorrupt body of the most holy Father
Cuthbert. Towards the end of the Queen's life he was continually with her, and with his prayers commended her soul
to Christ as it was leaving the body. Of her decease as he
saw it he more than once gave me a connected account, for I
often asked him, and he was wont to do so with tears.

29. " For a little more than half a year," he said, "she was
never able to sit on horseback, and seldom to rise from her bed.
On the fourth day before her death, while the King was absent
on an expedition, and at so great a distance that it was im-
possible for any messenger, however swift he might be, to bring
her tidings of what was happening to him that day, she became
sadder than usual, and said to me as I sat beside her: 'Perhaps
so great a calamity is to-day befalling the realm of Scotland
as has not overtaken it for many ages.' When I heard the
words I did not pay much attention to them ; but a few days
after a messenger came who informed us that the King had
been slain on the very day the Queen had spoken about them.
As if foreseeing the future, she had been very urgent with him
not to go with the army, but it chanced, I know not from what
cause, that he did not follow her advice.

30. " When the fourth day after the King's death approached,
her weakness having abated a little, she went into her oratory
to hear Mass, and there she took care to fortify herself beforehand for her departure, which was already at hand, with the holy

Viaticum of the Body and Blood of the Lord. Refreshed with this health-giving food, she went back to bed, for her former pains returned with greater severity. Towards the end her trouble increases and she was very sorely pressed. What can I do? Why do I delay? As if I were able to defer the death of my Queen, or lengthen her life—thus I fear to come to the end. But 'All flesh is grass, and all the glory thereof as the flower of the grass; the grass withereth and the flower falleth.' Her face had already grown pale with death when she directed that I and other ministers of the sacred Altar with me should stand beside her and commend her soul to Christ with our psalms. Moreover, she requested that a cross should be brought to her, called the Black Cross, which she had always held in the greatest veneration. But as the chest in which it was kept could not be quickly opened, the Queen said with a deep sigh: 'O unhappy that we are! O guilty that we are! Shall we not be permitted one last look of the Holy Cross!' When at length it was taken out of the chest and brought to her, she received it with reverence, and frequently tried to embrace it and kiss it, and to sign her eyes and face with it. Every part of her body was already growing cold, yet as long as the warmth of life throbbed in her breast she continued in prayer. She repeated the whole of the Fiftieth Psalm, and while so doing, placed the Cross before her eyes and held it there with both her hands.

31. 'It was whilst she was doing this that her son, who now after his father holds in this kingdom the helm of the State, arrived from the army and entered the Queen's chamber. What must then have been his distress? What his agony of soul? He stood there in a strait, with everything against him; whither to turn he knew not. He had come to announce to his mother that his father and brother had been slain, and he found his mother, whom he loved most dearly, at the point of death. Whom to lament first he knew not. Yet, the loss of his dearest mother, whom he saw lying almost dead before his eyes, pierced his heart with the sharpest pain. Besides all this, the condition of the kingdom was filling him with the deepest anxiety, for he well knew that disturbances would follow on

the death of his father. On every side he was met by sadness and trouble. The Queen when lying, as it seemed to those present, rapt in agony, suddenly collected her strength and addressed her son. She asked him concerning his father and his brother. He was unwilling to tell her the truth, lest if she heard of their death she herself would immediately die, and answered that they were well. But she, sighing deeply, said: 'I know it, my son; I know it. By this holy Cross, by the bond of our blood, I adjure thee to tell me the truth.' When he was thus pressed, he told her all as it had happened. What could she do, think you? Who would have believed that in the midst of so many adversities she would not murmur against God? At the same moment she had lost her husband and her son, and a disease had tormented her until she was on the point of death. But in all these things she sinned not with her lips, nor spoke foolishly against God, rather she raised her eyes and hands to heaven and broke forth into praise and thanksgiving, saying: 'Praise and thanks I give to Thee, Almighty God, that Thou hast been pleased that I should endure such great afflictions at my departing, and art pleased, as I trust, that, through enduring these afflictions, I should be cleansed from some stain of sin.'

32. "She now felt that death was close at hand, and at once began the prayer which is wont to be said by the priest after he receives the Body and Blood of our Lord, saying: 'Lord Jesus Christ, who, according to the will of the Father, through the co-operation of the Holy Ghost, hast by Thy death given life to the world, deliver me.' As she was saying the words 'Deliver me,' her soul was delivered from the chains of the body, and departed to Christ, the author of true liberty, whom she had always loved, and by whom she was made a partaker of the happiness of the saints, the example of whose virtues she had followed. With such tranquillity and such quietude was her departure, that there can be no doubt that her soul passed to the land of eternal rest and peace. It was remarkable that her face which, when she was dying, had exhibited the usual pallor of death, was afterwards suffused with red and white tints, so that it might have been believed that she was

not dead but sleeping. Her corpse was honourably shrouded as became a Queen, and we bore it to the Church of the Holy Trinity, which she herself had built; and there, as she had directed, we committed it to the grave opposite the Altar and the venerable sign of the Holy Cross which she had erected. And thus her body now rests in the place where she was wont to humble herself with vigils, prayers, shedding of tears, and prostrations."

THE LIFE OF S. MAGNUS.

THE LIFE OF S. MAGNUS.

PRAISE, glory, and honour with reverence be unto Almighty God, our Redeemer and Creator, for His manifold goodness and mercy which He has granted unto us, who dwell in the uttermost parts of the earth, and seem to the learned, as they have written in their books, as if we were utterly gone out from the world. Albeit, it has pleased God to show unto us His mercy ; especially in this, that he has suffered us to come to the knowledge of His blessed name, and therewith given us strong pillars, most saintly fore-runners of Holy Christianity by whose holiness all the Northern world shines and beams near and far. These are: the King, S. Olaf, and the illustrious Halward, his kinsman, who adorn Norway with their sacred relics; the worthy Magnus, Earl of the Isles, who illumines the Orkneys with his holiness, and to whose honour this history following has been composed. With these are the blessed Bishops, John and Thorlak, who have shed, with holy splendour, their illustrious merits upon Iceland. Wherefore it may be seen that we are not far off from the mercy of God, although our dwellings be placed far from those of other nations ; and therefore ought we to give thanks, honour, and reverence all the time of our life.

Master Robert, who has put together this history of the holy Earl Magnus and endited it in Latin, begins his prologue thus, as who will may hear :—

2. Such things as he is able each one brings to the tabernacle of God for help and mercy to himself: one gold, others silver, some precious stones, some goats' hair and red skins of he-goats ; and such offerings are not despised ; for of such is made the covering for the tabernacle of ·God, to shelter it and

protect it against moisture and the heat of the sun. These words may thus be glossed with a few words: Let every Christian man offer to God of the gifts and loans which he has granted him, the best he has: so that God's Christianity, which is the tabernacle, which Moses built for the service of God, signifies, that it may serve to defend and strengthen him against the assaults of his enemies. Gold signifies wisdom and knowledge; silver, chastity; precious stones, the miracles of the saints; goats' hair, the repentance of sin; the red skin of the he-goats, martyrdom. Now may the reader observe that all these offerings has S. Magnus offered to his Lord, as the story of his life bears witness. Now, although the praise of God may not be seemly in the mouth of sinful man, still it may be meet and helpful to others; for so we read that the whole house was filled with the sweetest perfume from the ointment and spices of the woman which was a sinner, who in penitence stooped down to wash and anoint the feet of the Lord. But after the wont of the men who till the fields of others but their own neglect and let lie dry, we begin this story of the life of the holy Earl Magnus with the greater confidence and love, and our labour spend upon so holy and noble a narrative, because we trust and fully expect his help to support and strengthen us to his own honour and glory. Now since he is a sharer in the kingdom of heaven and has entered into the kingdom of the Lord, he is able to obtain whatsoever he desires. But since we are sinful and may not, because of our wretched life, set of ourselves good examples to others, we show you the holy Magnus with his glorious life, whom all ought to follow, and take holy example from. Now that we may not be wearisome to the reader with this sermon (for the Lord made short sermons), we shall set forth this story in simple words and in pure speech as God gave us to perceive.

3. In the days of Harold Sigurd's son, King of Norway, there ruled over the Orkneys as Earls, two brothers, Paul and Erlend, the sons of Thorfinn, the most powerful of all the Earls of Orkney. He was son of Earl Sigurd whom King Olaf Tryggvi's son converted, along with all the people of the Orkneys, to the Christian Faith. This Sigurd fell at the

battle of Clontarf in Ireland. The mother of Erlend and
Paul was Ingibiorg, who was called Earlsmother, the daughter
of Earl Finn Arni's son. Harold Sigurd's son married Thora,
daughter of Thorberg Arni's son, and mother of Olaf the Quiet,
and therefore third cousins were King Olaf and the aforesaid
Earls. Earl Erlend married a woman called Thora, daughter
to Summarlid Ospak's son. Ospak's mother was Thordis,
daughter of Hall of Sida. Egill was the name of a son of the
aforenamed Hall ; his daughter was Thorgerd, the mother of
S. John, bishop of Holar. The sons of Earl Erlend and Thora
were S. Magnus and Erling, and daughters, Gunnhild and
Cecilia. Gunnhild was married afterwards to Kol Kali's son,
a franklin in Norway. Their son was Rognvald Kali, who
afterwards was Earl in the Orkneys ; he was a very holy man,
and sister's son to Earl Magnus the Saint. Earl Paul, Erlend's
brother, married a daughter of Earl Hakon, son of Ivar and
Ragnhild, daughter of King Magnus the Good, son of King
Olaf the Holy. Paul's son was called Hakon, who afterwards
comes into the story.

4. Earl S. Magnus was born in the Orkneys, the most noble
of race and illustrious of kindred. His father Erlend was
Earl of Orkney, a worthy lord and ruler, honoured for his
power and greatness, as is the wont of those who live magnificently in this world. His mother Thora was descended
from the most noble chiefs of this land. And though with
many greatness of birth is turned to pride and spoiling of
temper, yet was this blessed child already from the earliest
days of his childhood illuminated and instructed by the teaching of the Holy Spirit ; for he held to and loved, honoured
and preserved the highest virtue of the mind, a kindly nature,
and becoming manners, and steadfastness in honourable
ways. This boy showed himself old in good manners, share-
less in childish life in his deeds, glad spoken aud blithe, gentle
in his loving words, yielding and reasonable in his ways and in
all his behaviour ; well matured and staid, so that nothing was
found in his conduct to anger or offend men who beheld him.
At an early age he was sent to school, to learn the sacred
Scriptures and the other knowledge men then most studied to

know. Magnus was gentle and tractable, docile and obedient to his father and mother and teachers ; kind and dear to all the people. He attached himself little to wickedness and pastimes as other young men, but conducted himself in a seemly way, though he was young in the number of his years ; for there at once shone in him the manifest gift of the Holy Spirit, which guided him to all good things.

5. While the brothers, Erlend and Paul, held rule in the Orkneys, there came west from Norway King Harald Sigurd's son with a mighty army to the Orkneys, and left there Queen Elizabeth, and Mary and Ingigerd, his daughters. The earls resolved to accompany the King with a great army, and held them south to England : and in the battle they fought with King Harald Godwin's son, fell Harald Sigurd's son, the fifth night after S. Matthew's day, in the autumn. After this battle Olaf the Quiet, Harald's son, sailed with the earls that autumn back to the Orkneys. The same day and the same hour King Harald fell in England, died suddenly Mary, his daughter, in the Orkneys ; and the saying is that they had but one life between them. Olaf the Quiet passed the winter in the Orkneys, and was the best of friends with the Earls, his kinsmen, for brother's daughters were Thora, Olaf's mother, and Ingibiorg, the mother of the Earls. Olaf went in the Spring east to Norway, and was there made King with Magnus, his brother.

6. These brothers, Paul and Erlend, ruled the Orkneys a long time, and long was their agreement good. But when their sons began to grow up, Hakon and Erling became very overbearing, but Magnus was the quietest and best mannered in every thing. All the kinsmen were men of large stature, strong, and highly accomplished in all things. Hakon, Paul's son, wished to be overman to Erlend's sons, because he thought he was of better birth than they ; for he was daughter's son to Earl Hakon, Ivar's son, and Ragnhild, daughter of King Magnus the Good, as was before told, and he wished to have a greater share out of all their dealings. So it came about that they began not to agree ; for many men inclined to Erlend's sons, and would not have them to be inferior to any in the islands, for they

were of all the people better liked and beloved of men. This was a cause of great offence to Hakon all his life. The sons of the Earls were never safe with each other. Their fathers tried to arrange matters for them, that they might be at peace among themselves. A meeting was called, and it was soon found that each Earl favoured his own sons, and they began not to agree. Then great quarrels arose between these brothers, and so they parted. Next went men between them to make peace, and a meeting was called between them in Hrossey. At this meeting they were reconciled on this condition, that the Islands should be divided into two equal parts; and so things stood for a while. Hakon, Paul's son, greatly molested the men who served Erlend and his sons, so much so that it seemed to them that they could not endure it; and so they began to quarrel, and marched against each other with many men. Havard, Gunni's son, and other chiefs and friends of the Earls then tried to make peace between them, but Erlend and his sons would come to no agreement if Hakon was to remain in the Islands. But as it seemed to their friends that there would be great danger if they were not reconciled to each other, Hakon left the islands at once; and then an agreement was come to between those brothers on the advice of good men. Hakon first went east to Norway to see King Olaf the Quiet; it was towards the end of his days; he dwelt there a short time. Thence went he east to Sweden to see King Ingi, Steinkel's son, and was with him for some time well received. Christianity was then young in Sweden: many men were there who practised the old magic, and thought to become acquainted by it with many things which were not yet come to pass. King Ingi was a good Christian, and took great pains to root out the evils which had long attended heathenism.

7. When Hakon, Paul's son, was in Sweden, he heard tell that there was in the land a man who dealt in divination and spae-craft, whether it was by witchcraft or other means. Hakon was very anxious to meet this man, and to see what he could learn about his fate. He went in search of him and found him in a certain forest country, where he used to go about from feast to feast, and tell the franklins of the seasons and

other matters about which they were curious. When Hakon found this man he inquired of him how it would go with him for power or other fortune. The soothsayer asked him who he was. He tells him his name and family, that he was daughter's son to Earl Hakon, son of Ivar. Then answers the soothsayer: "Why wilt thou have knowledge or soothsaying of me? Knowest thou not that thy former kinsmen have had little faith in the kind of men that I am? And it may serve thy turn to try and learn thy fate from Olaf the Stout, thy kinsman in Norway, in whom all your faith is placed. But I suspect he will not stoop to tell thee that about which thou art curious, or else he is not so powerful as you call him." Hakon replied : "I will not speak ill of him : I think rather I am not worthy to get knowledge from him than that he should not be able to make me wise, if he would. But I have come to thee because it has come into my mind that neither of us will have need to look down upon the other because of virtue or religion." The man answers : "It likes me well to find that thou thinkest not to have all thy trust in that in which thy former friends had faith. It is strange also that the men who seek such things should keep fast and vigil, and think that thereby it will be given them to know the things about which they are curious. But though you apply yourselves to such, it turns out that you know less about them as your curiosity is greater and it is of the greater importance for you to know them ; but we put ourselves to no pains, and yet we are able to ascertain the things which it is important for our friends to know. Now it shall be thus between us two, thou shalt have this service from me as I see that thou thinkest thyself better able to get the truth from me than from King Ingi's priests, in whom it seems to him all his trust ought to be placed. Thou shalt come to me on the third night, we two shall then see whether I am able to tell thee some of the things thou art anxious to learn." After this they parted, and Hakon remained there in the district. And after three nights he came again to the soothsayer. He was then in a certain house alone, and breathed heavily when Hakon went in, and wiped his forehead, and said that he had had to struggle hard

before he became wise in the things he wanted to foreknow.
Hakon replied he would like to know what he had to tell.
He said then : " If thou wouldst know thy fate and about thy
life, it is long to tell : for from thy faring west to Orkney very
great events will come to pass when all the things to which
they lead are fulfilled. And I have a presentiment that thou
wilt become sole ruler of the Orkneys at last, though it
may be that to thee it will seem long to wait. I also think
that thy descendants will remain there. Thou wilt also in thy
days cause a crime to be done for which thou mayest, or mayest
not, get forgiveness from the God in whom thou trustest. But
thy steps lie further out into the world than I can see, yet I
think that thou wilt bring back thy bones to these northern parts.
Now have I told thee the things which at this time I am permitted, but thou wilt decide how thou wilt be content with thy
lot or errand." Hakon answered : " Great things thou tellest
me, if they be true ; but I think it will go better with me, as
it may well be that thou hast not seen these things in their
verity." The spaeman bade him believe what he liked of it.
And on this they parted.

And when Hakon had been a little while with King Ingi,
he fared thence to Norway to see King Magnus Bareleg, his
kinsman ; there he heard tidings from the Orkneys that Earl
Erlend and his sons ruled there most, and were in favour with
all the people, and that Earl Paul, his father, was caring little
about the government. It seemed to him also on inquiry, that
the Orkneymen were longing very little for his own return
home ; they had then good peace, and thought, if Hakon returned, discord and strife would arise. Also it seemed to
Hakon not unlikely that his own kinsmen would keep him out
of the government. He took counsel, therefore, to seek help
from his kinsman, King Magnus, to place him in the government of the Orkneys. Hakon egged on King Magnus greatly
to go a hosting to Scotland and Ireland and then to England
to avenge there King Harald, Sigurd's son. The King answers :
" Thou must bethink, thee, Hakon, if I did this at thy word,
and fared west with an army across the sea, whether it would
not take thee by surprise, if I put forward a strong claim to

those kingdoms beyond the sea, and did it without regarding the claim of any man." And when Hakon heard this, he grew cold and was little pleased, but King Magnus ordered a levy of men and ships over all Norway.

8. Now shall we next turn to the man about whom this history was written, the holy Magnus; for a little before you have heard how he was well-behaved in all his conduct and unlike to other young men in his growing up. But as it is the way with many to shape their conduct after that of those with whom they live, and he who touches pitch is defiled by it, so when Magnus had almost reached the fulness of his growth, placed in the midst of fierce and wicked men, who were ill-disposed towards good morals, infirm in faith, opposed to just laws, stiff-necked in learning, complaisant in evil ways, quarrelsome and disobedient towards the commandments of God, he seemed, for some winters, to be like wicked men, and as a viking with robbers or soldiers, he lived by rapine and spoil, and stood by with others at murders; and it is credible that he did this more from the wickedness and egging on of evil men than from his own badness. It seems likest to men that Magnus did this at the time when his kinsmen, Hakon and Erling, were all together in the Orkneys, for later no time can be found for it. Of this conduct, thus speaks Master Robert, who endited this history :—

"Ah! I marvel," he says, "how unspeakable is the depth of the riches of the divine wisdom and of the knowledge of God; how unsearchable are his judgments, and his ways past finding out by human kind. Why permitted Almighty God this His servant to lust after robbery and murder, and to be defiled with such manifold sins and misdeeds? Why tholed the divine clemency His knight and martyr to let himself fall so fearfully, who, from his birth, chose gloriously to crown him in heaven? With gladness and joy God enriched him, and turned his dust into heavenly glory, and gave him eternal joy after this world's sorrow, a garment of beauty and praise after the smitings of the heart. What is this? unless it be what we daily as openly as gloriously see, that God raises up and makes sons to Abraham from stones, just from unjust, honourable from sinners, glorious from mortal, smooth and polished, and four-cornered, with four main virtues, that they may be made to fit into the heavenly structure, strong and steadfast corner-stones in our chief corner-stone, Jesus Christ, they being of one heart and one mind with Him in the eternal charity and in the bond of infinite love. For the Lord Jesus is the son of the great Builder, who made the earth and all things which are therein, and creates and rules by His own power, and fashions vessels of His wrath into vessels of mercy, polishing them with the file of the Holy Spirit, and He receives sinful men into the widest bosom of His clemency and mercy, all who leave off their foolishness and turn to Him with their whole heart. For it belongs to the great glory and mercy of the Lord to let the abundance of His mercy appear there, where before the burden of our wretchedness was in the way, and he cures and heals the more mightily when the sickness already more fiercely assails the sick man, and makes whole all, and helps those who look to Him for help. See at last how the holy Magnus, though he was entangled in such sins, came to leave off these works and followed his father and brother and the landed men in Orkney."

9. At the time to which we have now come in the story, came west from Norway King Magnus Bareleg with countless ships and many troops. Him followed many of his vassals, Vidkunn Jonsson, Serk of Sogn, Kali of Agde, Saebjörn's son, and Kol, his son, and many other chiefs. The king intended, in this hosting, to subdue and harry the Western lands, England and Ireland, as was before said. When King Magnus came to Orkney, he took the Earls, Erlend and Paul, and drave them out of the islands and sent them East to Norway, and set Sigurd his son over Orkney, and gave him councillors, as he was not older than nine winters. Magnus and Erling, Erlend's sons, and Hakon, Paul's son, he ordered to go with him on the hosting. Magnus, Erlend's son, was tall in stature, bold and fleet and of great strength, of a goodly countenance, fair of complexion, and well shapen in limb, noble in bearing, and most courteous in all his demeanour. Him King Magnus made his table-swain, and he served continually at the King's table. King Magnus fared out of the Orkneys to the Hebrides and subdued in this

expedition all the Hebrides to his rule, and took prisoner Lawman, Gudrod's son, the king of the Hebrides. Thence fared he South to Wales and had there a great fight in the Menai Straits with two Welsh Earls, Hugh the Stout, and Hugh the Brave. But when men picked up their weapons, and got them ready for the fight, Magnus, Erlend's son, sat down in the forepart of the ship, where he was used to sit, and did not arm himself. The king inquired why he did so. S. Magnus answers: "Here I have nothing against any man, and therefore will I not fight." "Go, then," says the king, "below, and lie not here under men's feet, if thou dare not fight, for I do not think thou doest this because of thy religion." Magnus, the Earl's son, sat in the same place, and took a psalter and sang during the battle, but did not shelter himself. The battle was both hard and long. At last fell Hugh the Brave and the Welsh fled; and King Magnus got the victory, and had lost many good men, and many others were wounded. Kali, Saebjörn's son, received many and great wounds. Magnus, Erlend's son, was not wounded in the fight, though he did not shelter himself. And it might be seen of all, that it was the clearest miracle, that in so thick a flight of arrows, and so heavy a meeting of weapons, he should not be wounded, while on all sides around him fell armed men. And this need not now be wondered at, since God was preserving him for a greater crown and victory than to fall there. King Magnus was not pleased with this, and laid on Magnus, the Earl's son, great feud and dislike on account of it. And when the holy Magnus saw that it would not be for his honour or salvation to remain longer with King Magnus, he took another counsel with himself to do what God taught him.

10. It was one night, when King Magnus lay off Scotland, that Magnus, Erlend's son, stole away from the King's ship, and so arranged his bed, that it seemed as though a man lay there. In the morning, when the King was dressed, he inquired if Magnus, Erlend's son, were sick. He was then inquired for and was missed. The King then let search be made for him, but he was not found. Then the King caused the spoor-hounds to be let loose on the land. Magnus, the Earl's son, had hurt his

foot when he leapt ashore, and the spoor-hounds at once found the scent. Magnus had made for the woods and climbed up into a tree. The hounds came to the oak and climbed up into it. Magnus then struck one of them with a staff he held, and they immediately took to flight, laid their tails between their legs, and ran for the ships. Magnus, Erlend's son, hid himself in the wood while the King's men searched for him. He then fared up the country and came to the court of Malcolm, King of the Scots, and dwelt there for a while; but for some time he was in Wales with a certain bishop. The same autumn King Magnus fared back to the Hebrides, and was there through the winter. That winter died Kali, Saebjörn's son, of his wounds. Early in spring King Magnus fared to the Orkneys. There he heard from Norway of the death of the Earls; Erlend had died at Nidross and was buried there; and Paul at Bergen. Then King Magnus gave Gunnhilda, Earl Erlend's daughter, the sister of S. Magnus, in marriage to Kol, Kali's son, as an atonement for the life of his father, with many farms in Orkney. Kol was then made one of the King's vassals. Their son was Rognvald Kali. Some say that Erling, Erlend's son, and brother to S. Magnus, fell in the Menai Straits; but Snorri Sturlason says he fell in Ulster with King Magnus. For when King Magnus had ruled nine winters in Norway, he fared west to Ireland with a great army, and during the following summer fell in Ulster on Bartholomew's day. And Sigurd, his son, fared at once out of the Orkneys east to Norway, and was there made king along with his brothers Eystein and Olaf.

11. You have already heard in a former chapter how Almighty God is ready to show mercy, whose singular goodness is always to spare, and to turn hindrances into helps, and how He preserved this His chosen champion from the turmoils and dangers of the world, that he might reveal to him and show how great things it behoved him to suffer for His name's sake; and he who had often stood among great manslayers should at length become an offering of the Holy Spirit, and give to God his own blood with his life and body. Therefore came he out from the power of the greedy king, as was before read.

When the holy Magnus was in Scotland, he heard of the death of Earl Erlend, his father, and the other tidings which were before written. And when he had tarried as long in the Scots King's court as pleased him, honoured with the King's gifts and a noble retinue, he fared to Caithness, and there was well received, honoured and esteemed of all, and at once chosen and ennobled with the title of "Earl," beloved and honoured of all the friends of God.

12. Thereafter, without delay, the holy Earl Magnus was made Paul out of Saul, a preacher from a manslayer, and he avenged on himself that which he had lived ill. He began to bewail himself dead in sin with daily moanings and steadfast repentance; and he now took fitting revenge in manifold inflictions on the sinful lusts of the wretched flesh. He then showed himself a new man, as one who is inclined to that in which God is honoured and whom He has changed into another man, into good from evil, into seemly from sinful, into holy from defiled, into blessed and pure from polluted. This is the conversion of Thy right hand, O Almighty God! Thou art strong to strengthen, gracious to help, ready to restore, mighty to preserve! In this way was Magnus changed into a holy man. He began to ear the soil of his heart with the strong ploughshare of confession. Then slew he his man of misfortune and hid him under the sand. Then buried he the graven images of Laban under the roots of the trees. He tore out his sins and pollutions and adorned himself with illustrious virtues in good deeds after a godly manner with manlike steadfastness. He began then to flourish as an olive tree, and to be exalted in all good things and gracious works. Even as a cyprus excels other trees, so S. Magnus grew that he might be truly *magnus*; i.e., "great" in divine things as he was in name, increasing in prosperity and holiness.

13. A winter or two after King Magnus Bareleg fell, fared from the west over the sea to Norway, Hakon Paul's son, and the kings gave him the title of Earl, and such possessions as stood to him by birth. Fared he then west over the sea and took to himself all the government of the Orkneys, and with such great and aggressive greed that he slew without cause the

steward of the King of Norway, who held and governed that part of the Islands which the holy Magnus inherited, and in that way took possession of all the Orkneys by sheer force; for half of the Islands belonged to S. Magnus as his patrimony. Now when the holy Magnus heard with what violence Hakon, his cousin, had, with manifest injustice, seized his hereditary lands, he took counsel with his men as to what he should do. It was agreed among them that he should wait a while, in order that the anger and greed of Hakon, his kinsman, might abate, and that it might not appear that he sought his inheritance by arms, but as a friend and dear lover of law and justice.

14. Now when the time was come that the holy Magnus wished to visit his patrimony, he fares with a noble company from Caithness to Orkney, and his kinsmen and friends were fain of him. He asked to take possession of his patrimony. This was well pleasing to the franklins; for he was well loved; and he had many kinsmen and connections who were anxious to help him to hold his dominions. Thora, his mother, was then married to a man named Sigurd; they owned a large farm in Paplay. When Earl Hakon heard that Magnus was come into the Islands, he gathered troops around him, and wished not to give up the government, but to defend it. Fared then the friends of both between them, and tried to make peace. So it came to pass, through the counsel of good men, that they were reconciled on the condition that Earl Hakon should give up half the kingdom if it were so decided by the King of Norway. Magnus, Erlend's son, fared at once east to Norway to seek King Eystein; for King Sigurd had then fared out to Jerusalem. King Eystein received the young lord Magnus exceeding well, and gave up to him his patrimony, the half of Orkney, and therewith he received the title of Earl in the Orkneys from the Kings, along with very handsome presents. And after this fared the lord Earl Magnus west over the sea to his dominions, and his friends and kinsmen were glad and with them all the people. Then there was much good fellowship between him and Earl Hakon for many winters, which their friends brought about. There was then plenty and peace in the Orkneys while their friendship held. The kinsmen,

lord Earl Magnus and Hakon, had both the land defence together for a while, so that they were well agreed. So it was said in the songs, which were made on them, that they fought with the viking called Dufnial, who attacked their kingdom. He was a man one degree further off than first cousin to the Earls, and he fell before them. A man named Thorbjorn, rich and powerful by descent, but poor in good works, they, for sufficient reasons, put to death at Borgarfiord in Shetland. Many other things are also told in songs which they did together, though we cannot here minutely narrate them. The holy Magnus had these things done, not as a viking or robber, but as a just ruler of a province and a guardian of the laws, and a lover of peace, to chastise ill doing and to punish wrong, to make peace and quietness for his subjects and his kingdom against the violence and agression of wicked men, who were always on the watch to break the peace.

15. Lord Magnus was a man the most renowned in his rule and authority, dignified and upright, a steadfast friend and brave, skilled in feats of arms and blessed with victory in battle, gentle in peace, yet a strong ruler, condescending in speech, and clement, prudent in counsel, and had every man's praise. He was open-handed with his money, and generous among chieftains. Every day he gave great help to poor men for the love of God. He punished much harrying and theft, and caused vikings and ill doers, rich as well as poor, to be slain. No respecter of persons was he in his judgments ; he respected God's law more than differences of estate among them. In all things he observed strictly the commandments of God, and was unsparing towards himself. Many were the excellent virtues which he manifested before God, but hid from men.

But since the holy Earl Magnus had rule and government over worldly folk, he desired to be like the great ones of the earth in the customs of life ; he took and betrothed himself to a high-born princess, and the fairest maiden of the most noble house of the chiefs of Scotland, and brought her home with him and married her. This did the blessed Magnus, as experience proved, with the deep laid counsel of the divine mercy, to impose upon the enticing temptations

of this world, rather than to fulfil the lusts of the flesh, for he
was helped by divine protection and heavenly power. He
dwelt ten years with this virgin, pure and unstained of all the
pollutions of sin. And when he felt within himself the temptation to fleshly lust, he plunged into cold water and sought help
from God.

16. Behold this strong athlete of God in his daily wrestlings,
how wonderfully he lived with this maiden so long a time. For
although he lawfully might have enjoyed her, he preferred,
sustained by the mercy of the Holy Ghost, to chose the better
part, to live inviolate, than to do what is permitted in wedlock,
for they suffer the burning of the flesh who do such things.
Because better and safer is it to preserve the flowers whole
than to restore them after they are bruised; for no wound ever
becomes so well as the flesh which has remained whole. But
to live in the body without carnal lusts comes not of the power
of man, but of the Divine gift. But what temptation and
chastening he endured from the lust of the flesh, what heavy
blows of forbidden motives, and how hard a struggle he
conquered, and calmed the strong lusts of the burning flesh,
those know who have experienced them, but the inexperienced
believe not. Behold my dearest! This is the great sight which
Moses beheld when he saw the bush burning and not consumed;
that is to say, this young man was tempted but not overcome.
But, as says the Apostle Paul, no one is crowned except he who
strives lawfully and works manfully for it, so this prince and
wrestling knight preferred Thy courts, to endure the daily con-
flict and constant battle of the burning flesh. And he fought
valiantly and triumphed happily, for it seemed to him that he
would be much too easy a knight, who would have glory before
he had done works of virtue; for virtue is the way to glory,
and glory comes from virtue. Treacherous is the glory, and
vain is the beauty which is not begotten by holy virtue. And
I marvel, says the Scripture, how fair and winsome is the immaculate conception with its purity and love. This the glorious
knight of God, girt with his girdle of chastity, was careful with
all mindfulness to do and fulfil all manner of charity to the
glory of his Lord. But what of the things of this world would

he deny his God, who expended his very life and body, and poured out his own blood for the sake of God?

17. Now since no one can be an Abel unless he suffer and experience the ill-will and malice of Cain, and the holy Ezekiel dwelt among men full of the poison of adders, and just Lot was oppressed by unjust men, the enemy of all mankind stirred up temptations and hot persecutions on every side against this knight of God, sowing discord and hatred among brethren and kinsmen and dear friends, all to hinder him, and to bring to naught his good deeds, which then began to increase with him; but the branch of the good vine might be moved, but not cut off. For as wood swims in water and is turned over by the winds and waves, but not sunk, and as the Wain turns round in the heavens, and sinks not, as gold is purified in the furnace and is not consumed, and as a strong house is beaten upon by the storms and falls not; so in the same way was the mind and heart of this noble martyr strong and steadfast, undaunted and undismayed amid the fierce trials and onsets of manifold temptations, in the midst of storms and great breakers both of secret envy and treachery, as well as of open ill-will and spite, against the shafts of the tempting foe. It must next be set down how this discord was made between the Earls.

18. When the kinsmen, S. Magnus and Earl Hakon, had for some winters ruled their lands in peace and good agreement, it came to pass, as it often does, that evil disposed men began to destroy their brotherly concord. Earl Hakon then drew towards those evil men, for the kinsmen were very unlike in temper. Lord Earl Magnus was benevolent and faithful in his promises; he wished to retain the kingdom which God had given to him, and desired nothing more. For in what way could he be proved to desire other men's kingdoms or possessions, who was so free with his own flesh, that he did not spare his life for the love of God? He reformed his subjects and accustomed them to right living, so that after he had delivered and given peace to his kingdom from the aggressions of wicked vikings, he did not allow any of his men to go a hosting, and punished severely all lawlessness and wickedness. But Earl

Hakon was hard-hearted and cruel, greedy both of wealth
and power, and more prone to egg on his men to go a hosting
than to prevent them, and punished little wickedness and
ill-doing. He was very jealous of the liberality and popular
favour of the holy Magnus, and would willingly with the
greed of his evil counsellors overcome the honour of Earl
Magnus, and subdue his kingdom to himself with pillage and
injustice, and began to plot with his men against his life with
treacherous cunning.

19. Now when the blessed Magnus has become thoroughly
aware of this through much experience, which he thinks cannot
be passed over in silence, that Hakon was attempting to deprive
him of his life and kingdom, he took counsel with his counsellors, and it seemed to them that he ought to give way for a
little to the malice and fury of Hakon. Chose he then out of
his people those who were the most suitable and best of his
followers to accompany him, and sailed to England and sought
a meeting with King Henry, son of William the Bastard, who
was then sole king over England. When the holy Magnus
was come to this King, he made known to him the occasion
and object of his coming. And the King received him with
great honour ; and into so great a friendship did he rise with
the King, that he maintained him and all his people at his own
cost for twelve months magnificently, as it was fitting for a
King to treat a famous leader. But this holy martyr held
himself and his retinue so wisely, that he shunned and was
wary of all fellowship with wicked men. And when the lord
King learned from his prudence, how Earl Magnus was a doer
of good works and of seemly manners, and that the Holy Spirit
dwelt in him, he earnestly gave heed to his counsel, and
followed his advice in his conduct, for he was sound and
wholesome in counsel and in making of plans, of
gentle disposition and patient as Chusa, gladsome and loving
as Jonathan, just and zealous for the law as Phinehas. Hence
he was dear to all and beloved, pleasant, and acceptable, so that
there were many who said : " Blessed are they that saw thee,
and that won thy friendship." He was pleasant and kind
to the rich, open-handed and gentle with the poor, good

natured, benevolent, and condescending to all the people.
And although he dwelt at the Court with the princes of this
world, he took care and avoided all kinds of vice which corrupt
the manners of courtiers. And that he might not for the
future stain his chastity by consenting to other men's sins, he
made ready his home-going as soon as the twelve months
were passed, which he had spent with King Henry. It may be
that God had made known to him that he should finish his
labours within a short time, and offer to God as well the bright
flowers of his purity as the victorious death of his martyrdom ;
for to be loosed from the body, and to live with Christ, is much
more glorious than to abide here in this polluted world.

20. After that S. Magnus had taken leave of King Henry,
honoured with rich and manifold gifts, and esteemed and
glorified by the Lord King, they parted with the greatest
love and friendship. He visited first all the holy places which
were near, and then fared home to his own land. But while
the holy Magnus was abroad, Earl Hakon with great greed and
harrying had subdued not only all the Orkneys, but all Caithness as well, with great robbery and violence ; and so it
came to pass, that Hakon sat at that time in Caithness, when
the holy Earl Magnus landed in the Orkneys with five ships
well manned with valiant and well armed men, ettling to
get back his kingdom, though with no false passion of this
world's ambition, nor greed of unlawful possession, especially
when he had already so long desired God, and was with the joy
of his whole heart wholly taken up out of the lusts of mortal
things into the desire for eternal joy, for he came now to end
his long life into a brief space all the more gloriously the
more quickly he departed. The tidings of his return home
were at once told on all sides. Earl Hakon, immediately
awaking as a fierce she-bear robbed of her whelps, summoned and gathered together to him the sons of Belial, cruel ill-
doers, and sons of the wretched Dohet, who always and everywhere wrought evil from their birth from their mother's womb.
Hakon meant then to come unawares upon the holy Magnus,
and to work and complete in that way the malice and treachery
which he had long before had in mind and prepared for. But

the Supreme Heavenly King, who from eternity had ordained
that He would keep His glorious chosen vessel in His treasuries,
saw in this man of His own election some rust still of worldly
behaviour which required to be purified. Therefore God
would that he should be made most pure and fair in a few days
with the fire of suffering and insult, and with the files of
temptation and of many adversities, though there was no
deadly sin in him to wash away. God wished to increase his
merit, if in anything it was lacking, that according as his
temptation and wrestling were greater and harder, the higher and
more splendid should be the glory and joy of the victor. Thus it
came to pass that the Earls sent between themselves with mes-
sages for peace and reconciliation their most prudent counsellors, who truly bear the marks of Chusa and Ahitophel,
who brought about the reconciliation between King David
and his son Absolom, when they were at variance. It came
then at last in this matter, through the intervention of good
men, that a reconciliation was made between the kinsmen in
this way, that the earldom of Orkney, Caithness, and Shetland should be divided into halves between the Earls Magnus
and Hakon, and that neither should assail the other's kingdom
with any greed. When this agreement had been made and confirmed with oaths and handsellings, the Earls met with the kiss
of peace. But that which the holy Earl Magnus intended for
peace, Hakon turned to deceit and cunning. And the longer
he retained the poison of evil, the more wickedly did he spew
it up, for his wickedness and villainy increased so much as
time went on, that he could no longer hide it. In the same
way as a cancer on the face of a man works the more harm the
longer it remains, so fares every kind of evil ; thus, the longer
it is hid in the mind and heart, the fiercer it becomes for
working mischief.

21. The holy Earl Magnus then began again to rule his kingdom
with peace and joy for a time. And it is known best in the sight
of God how holily he lived in this biding of his death ; how he
adorned himself with holy virtues and the exercise of every
kind of grace, in prayer, and in shedding of tears, and search-
ings of heart, in purity and nobleness, in alms-giving, and in

all gentleness towards his people, in afflictions and manifold sufferings, which he endured in his body, and in many other virtues more than sinful man can call to mind. As every holy man of God does, in the same way prepared Earl Magnus for his martyrdom ; the story of which we shall now with God's help begin.

22. When the above mentioned reconciliation and peace had lasted between the Earls some winters, Hakon showed himself traitorous by pouring out from his breast the great wickedness, which he had for a time held back. Hear how true is that saying of the ancient skald, which says :

> " Nulla fides regni sociis, omnisque potestas,
> Inpatiens consortis erit, totum sitit illa."

That is to say : Never can fellowship in this world's power be true, for no ruler can endure a rival, and would have all to himself alone. From this thou mayest learn what fruit treason begets and what springs up from greed. All sins are done of lust, and every unhallowed desire starts from greed. This is proved by Ahab, that most iniquitous king, who persecuted Elijah the prophet. It is shown by the most wicked Judas, who sold our Lord for money. This same, the traitor, Earl Hakon, showed, both by examples and proofs in the treachery with which he betrayed his kinsman, Earl Magnus, under the show of friendship, though in various ways happened the things which led to their dealings and quarrel.

23. Two men were with Earl Hakon who are mentioned as by far the worst in going between the kinsmen ; the one was called Sigurd ; the other Sigvat Sokki. Sigurd had a brother, called Thorstein, who was the most faithful follower of Earl Magnus. Many others there were who had an evil hand in this matter, and these were all with Hakon, for S. Magnus would keep no slanderer among his followers. These slanderings went so far that the Earls gathered their troops together, and each fared against the other with a great following. They both held their way to the island of Hrossey, for there was the Thingstead of the Orkneys. And when they were come there, each of them drew up his troops in battle array and prepared

to fight. There had come all the men of rank with the Earls, and many were friends of both, who did everything to reconcile them, and went between them with courage and good-will. This meeting was in Lent. And because many well disposed men were anxious to prevent strife between them, and wished to help neither to do harm to the other, they bound themselves to keep the peace by oaths and handsellings at the witness of the best men. It was settled they should meet in the spring in Egilsey after Easter. At this meeting each Earl was to have two ships and an equal number of men. Both Earls took oaths to have and hold the agreement which the best men should settle at that meeting to declare between them. And after this was done each fared to his own home. With this conditional reconciliation and agreement the holy Magnus was well pleased, as he was thoroughly whole hearted and of good conscience, without all distrust. But Earl Hakon had at this meeting glosed over his treachery and hid it with a cloud of hypocrisy; for this agreement he had made with deceit and treachery and complete fraud, as was afterwards proved; for at the time Hakon, who is rightly called a treasury of hidden evil, and his wicked servants conspired together in the counsel of their wickedness for the slaughter and death of the holy Magnus. For strong and very dear is all evil amid the fellowship of the scornful; therefore settled they among themselves that this crime should no longer be delayed, and that now will they fully slake their cruel thirst with the shedding of sackless blood. But the Highest Lord of all power watched over his beloved friend and chosen martyr, that being at this time ready for the kingdom of heaven, he might be taken out of this life under the heavy storm of a violent death; as grapes under the winepress, trodden upon and crushed, give off the clearest wine in their time with much fragrance and sweet taste, so gave this the glorious martyr of God, by his death, to all the friends of God and his own, the heavenly sweetness of divine mercy, from that glory and joy which he has inherited in the unending gladness of eternal life with God and his saints.

24. As soon as the holy Easter time was passed, each of the two made ready for this meeting in different ways. The holy

Magnus called to him all the men whom he knew had the most good-will to make things better between the kinsmen. He had two longships manned with the bravest men, as many as were agreed upon. And when he was ready he held to the island of Egilsey. But as they were rowing on a calm sea and in still weather, there rose a wave of the sea beside the ship in which Earl Magnus was, and broke over the place where the Earl was sitting. The chief men in Earl Magnus's ship were called : Thorstein, who was mentioned before, Arnkell, Grim, and Gilli, and many other doughty men. They marvelled greatly at this circumstance, that the wave fell on them in a calm sea, where no man knew that a wave had fallen before, and where the water under was deep. Then the holy Earl Magnus said : " It is not strange though you wonder at this. But my thought is, that this is a foreboding of the end of my life. Maybe that will happen here, which was before spaed, that Earl Paul's son will perpetrate the greatest crime : maybe Hakon is plotting treachery against us at this meeting." Earl Magnus's men were much distressed at this speech when he spoke of so speedy expectation of his death, and prayed him to take care of himself and guard his life, and risk nothing to the faith of Earl Hakon. Earl S. Magnus replies : " I shall certainly go to this meeting, as was agreed upon, and make no breach of my promise for the sake of a mere foreboding. And let all be as God wills about our voyage. But if there be any choice, then would I much rather suffer wrong than do it to another. So may God let Hakon, my kinsman, get forgiveness, though he do me wrong."

Now it is to be told of Earl Hakon, that he called to him a great army. He had seven or eight warships, all of great size, manned with troops; all the men were well armed as if they were going to battle. But when the force came together, then did Earl Hakon make it clear before his men, that at this meeting it should be so settled with Magnus, that they should not both rule from that time forth. Many of the Earl's men, who might verily be called children of the devil, expressed delight at this purpose, and added many abominable words; but Sigurd and Sigvat Sokki were still giving the worst advice ; they were ever egging on to wickedness. The men

then began to row fast, and went furiously and with great
speed. Havard Gunni's son, who was spoken of before, was
with Earl Hakon; he was a close friend of both Earls. Hakon
had hid from him this bad counsel. But as soon as he was
aware of it, he leapt overboard from the Earl's ship and swam
to an uninhabited island; for he would be in no treachery
with Hakon against the holy Magnus. That man was with
Earl Magnus, who was called Holdbodi, a trustworthy franklin
from the Hebrides; he was Earl Magnus's most dear follower.
He was near by all that happened, and has since most clearly
related the dealings and all the discourse of Earls Hakon and
Magnus, which may here be heard next after this.

25. The holy Earl Magnus came sooner to Egilsey with his
men than Hakon. And when they saw Hakon's eight warships, Earl Magnus thought he knew that treachery was being
prepared, and all the men, who had any insight saw well
that such a multitude of armed men was not wanted for a
peaceful purpose. When the holy Earl Magnus saw that the
treachery of Hakon was about to show itself, he went with his
men up into the island to a church to pray, and was there
through the night, not because of fear or dread, but rather to
commit all his care to God. His men offered to defend
him, and fight against Hakon. But he answered: "I will
not place your lives in danger for me. And if peace cannot be made between us two kinsmen, then let it be as God
wills; for rather will I suffer evil and treachery than do it to
others." For this noble martyr, when saying this, knew that
all guile and deceit is returned to him who does it. Now
thought his men most true that which he had before said to
them about the treachery of Hakon. But as Earl Magnus
knew before of his death, whether it were of his foresight or
of divine revelation, he wished neither to fly nor to go far from
the meeting of his enemies, and he went for no other reason to
the holy church than for religion. Earl Magnus watched long
in prayer during the night and meditated on his salvation, and
prayed earnestly; he committed all his cause and himself into
the hands of God. In the morning he let Mass be sung, and
received in that Mass the *Corpus Domini*. And this his deed

was necessary for the highest reason, that in that place he should become an offering to God, as was offered the redeeming sacrifice of the Body and Blood of our Lord Jesus Christ for the salvation of the whole world. But Earl Hakon, who at that time was void of all piety and affection, violating the privileges of the Church, feared not to go into the holy sanctuary, so breaking its peace and immunity, that he might show his wickedness the more fiercely, the more sacred the place he perpetrated it in. For sin is ever increased by ill-doing, and evil by outrage ; and sinful man, when he falls into the depths of sin, abandons all fear of God ; and the more he is acquainted with sin the more he dares, and the less he cares what ill he does ; for he thinks it is nothing worth, however great his misdeeds be. The same morning that Earl Hakon had come up on to the island with his ill-doers, he sent four of his men, the worst of his servants, who were the fiercest and most eager to work ill, to seize Earl Magnus wherever he was. These four, who, from their ferocity, may rather be called the wildest wolves than rational men, always thirsting for bloodshed, leapt into the church just as Mass was ending. Snatched they at once the holy Earl Magnus with great violence, uproar, and clamour, out of the peace and bosom of Holy Church, as the gentlest sheep of the fold.* The Saint was holden of the thralls of sin, the righteous was bound, dragged unjustly by the unjust, and then led away before the greedy judge, Earl Hakon. But this strong champion had such great steadfastness in all these wrestlings, that neither his body shook from fear, nor his mind from dread or grief, for he forsook this thorny world with all its fruitless flowers. He hoped that God would recompense his patience

---

* The Shorter Saga gives a different account. "Next morning he went out of the Church with two men out on the island down to the shore to a certain hiding-place, and prayed there before God. Some men say that Earl Magnus caused mass to be said for him before he went out from the Church and that he took the *Corpus Domini*. Earl Hakon and his men ran up on the island in the morning, and first to the church, and sought for Earl Magnus, and did not find him there. Then they searched for him about the island. But when Earl Magnus saw where they were, he called to them and said " Here I am." And when Hakon saw that, they ran thither. Cc. 11, 12.

with an ineffable crown ; but their cruelty and fury with everlasting torture in the hot fire of hell, because of their inhuman wickedness and monstrous greed.   He was as glad and cheerful when they took him, as if he had been bidden to a banquet, and had so settled a heart and mind that he spoke to his enemies with no bitterness, anger, or tremor in his voice.

26. When the holy Earl Magnus was come before Earl Hakon, he said to Hakon with great calmness : " Not well doest thou, kinsman, when thou kept not thy oath, and it is much to be looked for that thou didst this more from the malice and egging on of others than from thine own ill-will.   Now I will make to thee three offers, that thou mayest take one of them rather than that thou shouldst break thy oath, and let me thy kinsman be slain, sackless as some will say." Earl Hakon said: " I will first hear what thou offerest."   S. Magnus said : " This is the first offer, that I shall fare abroad to Rome or all out to Jerusalem, to seek the holy places, and so make atonement for both of us ; I will take two ships out of the land furnished with good men and the equipment needful to have.   I will swear never to come to Orkney again."   This offer was quickly refused by Hakon and his men.   Then said Earl Magnus : " Now since our life is in your power, and I know that in many things I have offended against Almighty God, and have need thereof to make amends, send me up to Scotland to the friends of us both, and let me there be in ward with two men with me for amusement ; and see thou so to it that I may never come forth of that wardship without thy leave."   This they at once rejected and found many reasons why it could not be.   Then spake this doughty knight : " Now is my choice very limited, says he.   Now is there but one choice left, which I will offer thee, and God knows that I am more concerned for thy salvation here, than for the life of my body ; for, after all, it beseems thee little to take my life.   Let me be maimed in my limbs, or let my eyes be put out, and set me so in a dark dungeon, whence I may never come out."   Then said Earl Hakon : " This offer take I, and no more do I ask."   Then leapt up Earl Hakon's men and said : " In this finding we do not agree, to torture Earl Magnus : but one or the other of

you two we will slay; and from this day you shall not both of
you reign over these lands." Then says Earl Hakon: "Rather
will I rule the lands than die at once, if ye are so strict in this
matter." So tells Holdbodi of their parley.—After this S.
Magnus fell to prayers and bowed his face into his hands and
shed many tears before God, giving his cause, his life, and himself, into the power of the Lord.

27. Next to this, when the holy friend of God, Earl Magnus,
was condemned and doomed to death, Earl Hakon bade Ofeig,
his standard-bearer, slay Earl Magnus; but he refused with
greatest anger. Then compelled Earl Hakon his cook, who
was called Lifolf, to smite Earl Magnus, but he began to weep
aloud. Then said Earl S. Magnus to him : "Weep not; for
there is fame to thee in doing the like. Be thou of steadfast
mind, for thou shalt have my clothes as is the wont and law
of the men of old. Thou shalt not be afraid, for thou doest
this by force, and he that forces thee to it has more sin
than thou." And when he had said this, he took off his
kirtle and gave it to Lifolf. Then begged the blessed Earl
Magnus leave to pray first, and it was granted him. He fell
then to the ground and gave himself into the power of God,
offering himself to Him in sacrifice. Not alone for himself prayed
he, but rather for his enemies and murderers as well; and
forgave he them all with his whole heart that which they were
misdoing against him ; and confessed he all his sins to God,
and prayed that they might all be washed away by the shedding of his blood ; and he commended his spirit into the hands
of God, praying God's angels to come to meet it, and bear
it to the rest of Paradise. Then when this noble martyr
of God had ended his prayer, he said to Lifolf : "Stand before
me and hew me on the head a great wound ; for it beseems
not to behead chiefs like thieves. Be strong, man, and weep not,
for I have prayed God to pardon thee." After this Earl Magnus
crossed himself, and bowed him to the stroke. Lifolf struck
him on the head a great blow with an axe. Then said Earl
Hakon : "Strike again." Then struck Lifolf into the same
wound. Then fell the holy Earl Magnus on his knees, and
fared with this martyrdom from the miseries of this world to the

everlasting joys of the kingdom of heaven. And him whom the murderer took out of the earth, Almighty God let reign with Him in heaven. His body fell to the earth, but his spirit was gloriously taken up into the heavenly glory of the angels. The spot where the holy Earl Magnus was slain was stony and mossy. But a little after his merits before God were made manifest, so that since then there is there a green field, fair and smooth, and God showed by this token, that Earl Magnus was slain for righteousness sake, and gained the fairness and greenness of Paradise in the land of the living.—The death-day of the holy Earl Magnus is two nights after the feast of Tiburtius and Valerianus; it was on the second day of the week, that the worthy Earl Magnus was slain, the third week after Lady Day in Lent. He had then been twelve winters Earl with Hakon. Then were Kings in Norway Sigurd the Crusader, and his brothers Eystein and Olaf. Then had passed from the death of the holy Olaf, Harald's son, seventy-four years [eighty-six]. It was in the days of Pope Paschal, the second of that name, and of S. John Bishop of Holar in Iceland.—In honour of the holy Earl Magnus thus speaks Master Robert who in Latin this history endited :

28. "To-day shines upon us, dearest brethren, the day of the death of the blessed Earl Magnus the Martyr, the day of his rest and of his eternal joy. Let us be glad and rejoice on this glorious day; for he requires of us solemn devotion and especial thanksgiving, who live beside his holy relics and under his protection and keeping, and have hope in his merits. For it was on account of his noble example and holy life that first flourished in the coasts of the kingdom of the Orkneys the seemly ordinances of pure devotion, and the most holy laws of this most glorious martyr brought forth manifold fruit in good living. He drave abroad the lordly throne of Satan out from the northern regions of the world and set in its place the tabernacle of Almighty God. He laid waste and uprooted all the tares by his preaching, and let spring up the fairest flowers and the sweetest harvest of most life-giving fruit. He turned all the bitterness of the Orkneys into praise and sweetness of holy living. On this day he overcame the

world and the princes of the world, and he went up, a radiant
conqueror over the world, receiving from his holy Master, our
Lord Jesus Christ, a crown of glory.   On this day he was
set free from all bondage of fleshly corruption, entering into
heaven ; and he went into joy, made like the saints in all
glory.   On this day he laid aside the earthly garments of this
changeful life, and went up higher than human weakness may
reckon ; and on him therefore is bestowed greatness in heaven,
honour and blessedness in the presence of all the saints.   He
ascended radiant according to his merits, rich in the fulness of blessing, glorious in noble victories.   This glorious
martyr of God, the blessed Earl Magnus, adorned with the
crown of his own blood, suffered after the incarnation of our
Lord Jesus Christ, one thousand one hundred and four [six-
teen] years, on Monday the sixteenth of the kalends of May.
Now it remains, my dearest brethren, that we lay aside fleshly
lusts and beware of loving unlawful things, vanquishing and
overcoming the assaults of sin, and follow the footsteps and
life of this glorious martyr with all the strength of our mind as
far as our weakness will allow.   Let us follow the way of his
life ; let us hold to the example of his works.   Let us strive to
make our lives like his, though it daily appeareth and is
shown forth—by those wonderful tokens and glorious works
which Almighty God doth grant unto the North both by sea
and land for the sake of his excellent prayers and famous
merits—that his life and holy righteousness are things more
meet for us to honour and wonder at than to be imitated
by our weakness.   He appeared on earth, that he might become
our protector and ask help and grace for us from Almighty
God.   Therefore it behoves us, who are pressed down under the
great load of our sins, honour always to do to him with the
especial goodness of bounden obedience and honour, that this
glorious martyr, Earl Magnus, may vouchsafe to obtain for us,
by means of his merits and prayers, that we may win to become sharers of his victorious crown and eternal glory, which
he won on the day of his passion.   This grant us the Lord
Jesus Christ, who is the honour and blessing, the help and salvation, the gladness and glory of all His holy and righteous men ;

who with the Father and Holy Ghost liveth and reigneth, One God in Three Persons, world without end. Amen."

Master Robert wrote this history in Latin to the worship and honour of the holy Magnus, Earl of the Isles, when twenty years were gone from his passion.

29. Now must we take up the story again, and tell of the things which were done after the death of the holy Earl Magnus. So great was the fierceness and cruelty of Earl Hakon, and so great his anger and fury at the blessed Magnus, that he bore not less malice to Earl Magnus dead than living. And though the anger and fury of most men can be abated after the doing of their ill deed, the ill will and malice in the heart of Hakon took no rest and abated not ; for he forbade Earl Magnus to be buried at the Church as Christian men, but ordered that he should be hidden there in the ground where he was slain.

30. It had been agreed at the first meeting of the Earls in Hrossey, that when their reconciliation had been fully made and confirmed as the best men determined, as they had bound themselves by oaths, that both Earls, when they fared from the meeting, which was fixed to be held in Egilsey, should go to a feast in Paplay at Thora's, the mother of Earl Magnus. But now, after the slaying and death of the Earl, went Earl Hakon to the banquet with his men. The feast was of the best. Now when drink took hold on Earl Hakon, then went Thora to him and spake thus: "Now art thou come here alone, lord ; but I expected both of you, thee and Earl Magnus my son. Now be thou so to my prayer as thou wilt that Almighty God shall be to thee at doomsday ; that thou grant to me that my son may be buried at church." Earl Hakon looked on her, and shed tears, and said : " Bury thy son, woman, where it likes thee." Earl S. Magnus was then borne to the church, and buried in Birsay, at Christ's Kirk, which Earl Thorfinn, his grandfather, let be built. Immediately a heavenly light was often seen to shine over his grave. Then men began to call upon the holy Earl Magnus, when they were placed in danger, and he met their need as they prayed. Always was a heavenly odour perceived at his grave, and there sick men obtained health.

Next, sick men made journeys from Orkney and Shetland, who were hopeless of cure, and watched before his tomb, and were cured of all their diseases, but still men did not dare to make known the miracles of Earl Magnus while Earl Hakon lived. So it is told, that the men who had been worst between the Earls and most in treachery towards Earl Magnus, came most of them to speedy ends and short life, and died a shameful death.

After the death of Magnus, Hakon, Paul's son, took possession of all the Earldom of the Orkneys. He compelled all men to swear oath and fealty to himself, as well those who before had served Earl Magnus. He became great, and laid heavy burdens on the friends of Earl Magnus, whom he thought had been most against himself in their negotiations. Some winters after, Hakon made ready to go abroad. He went south to Rome, and on that journey went all the way to Jerusalem, as was then the custom for palmers. He sought the holy places, and bathed in the river Jordan. After that he returned to his own land and took up the government in the Orkneys. He became then a good ruler, and established good peace in his kingdom. He made new laws, which the franklins liked much better than those which had been before. By such things he began to increase his popularity. So it came to pass that the people of the Orkneys would have no other than Earl Hakon and his offspring to hold rule among them. And here is the end of what is to be said about Hakon in this book.

31. The most merciful God, our Lord Jesus Christ, who invites and leads His friends to everlasting joy, from all the bondage of this world, . . . the same who redeems all who humble themselves to His mercy, with their whole heart, from all the sins and pollutions of this sorrowful world, and makes of the ignorant the wisest, of the lowly and despised the most famous, of the poor the richest, of the ignoble the noblest rulers, not only of the kingdoms of this world, but also of the kingdom of heaven, and of eternal glory, as He did aforetime with the patriarch Joseph, who was led out of a dark dungeon and at once made prince and ruler over all the land of Egypt : the

same who made of the shepherd boy, David, the greatest king over all the tribes of Israel, and led Judas Maccabæus out of the famine of the desert, that he might obtain honour and the renown of victory, and so great a fame that in many things he is thought to far excel others, and Alexander, the son of Philip, who was called the Macedonian, because of the hard mastership of Aristotle * .   .   .   .   .

15. At this time William was bishop in the Orkneys. Then was the bishop's seat at Christ's Kirk in Birsay where the holy Earl Magnus was buried ; he doubted long about his holiness and kept down this new thing [*i.e.*, the miraculous virtue experienced at the grave of S. Magnus, c. 30.]

16. Bergfinn, Starri's son was the name of a franklin north in Shetland. He was sightless, and fared south to the Orkneys and watched at the tomb of the Earl S. Magnus. With him watched two men, one was named Sigurd and the other Thorbjorn ; they were both cripples. Earl S. Magnus appeared to them all and made them quite cured. Again twenty-four men watched at the tomb of Earl Magnus and all got healing for their hurts.

Many men told this before Bishop William and urged him to speak about it with Paul, Hakon's son, who then ruled over the Isles after his father, and ask him to give leave that the sacred relics of Earl Magnus might be taken up out of the ground, but the bishop took that heavily. Often was he reminded in dreams that he should make up his mind about the Earl's holiness, and yet he would not believe in it. Afterwards it so came about that he was beaten with divine scourges that he might honour the tokens and holiness of Earl Magnus.

17. One summer Bishop William sailed East to Norway on some pressing business, and immediately turned homewards in the autumn, and came in the beginning of winter to Shetland. There he was laid up by contrary winds and storms. But when for a long time during the winter there was no fair

---

* The following paragraphs are taken from the Lesser Saga in order to fill up the gap which occurs here in the Greater Saga.

wind for the isles, the Bishop despaired of being able to reach
his see before spring.   The captain asked him if he would
agree to the holiness of Earl Magnus if he should sing mass
the next Lord's Day at home.   The bishop, so to say, gave
his consent to this, but more from necessity than of free
promise.   But when this was agreed, there was calm weather
and soon a fair wind.   And afterwards they sailed for Orkney ;
and he came home also before the next Lord's Day ; and all
praised God and also his holy martyr Earl Magnus.   Some
men say this, that Bishop William did not agree to take out
of the ground the sacred relics of Earl Magnus before it happened there at home one day at a time that he could not get
out of the church.   For he had become blind and could not
find the door, till he repented of his unbelief, and wept bitterly,
and besought God that he might light upon the tomb of Earl
Magnus.   And when he came there, he fell all his length on
the ground, and promised to at once take out of the earth his
sacred relics, when he received his sight.   And when he had
ended his prayer, he received his sight there at the tomb.

18. Afterwards he summoned the wisest and the best men
in Orkney, and there came a great multitude to Christ's Kirk
at Birsay.   Then were taken out of the ground the sacred
relics of Earl Magnus, and then the bones were almost come
up out of the ground.   He then let wash the bones, and the
joint of the finger to be taken and tested in the consecrated
fire thrice.   But it burnt not, rather it became like burned
silver.   Some men said it ran into the form of a cross.   Then
there were many miracles done by the holy relics.   After that
took learned men the holy relics and laid them in a shrine, and
set them over the altar.   That was on Lucy's day [December
13] before Yule; and then there had passed twenty years since
the slaying of Earl Magnus.   The day of his death is holden in
spring, the sixteenth of the kalends of May [April 16].   Bishop
William directed the festival to be held on either of the two days
over all his bishopric ; and he was afterwards in great love with
the holy Earl Magnus.   William was the first bishop in Orkney, and ruled sixty-six years.

* . . and prepared in every respect as becomingly as possible.
Then enshrined the lord Bishop the holy relics of the blessed
Earl Magnus with honour and reverence and the hymns of all the
people, and there were healed all who were lacking health, and
in need of pity, who at that time had thither sought his sacred
relics. Earl S. Magnus was enshrined on the Feast of the
Virgin Lucy, before Yule in the winter. And that day is
widely held in veneration both for the holy Magnus and God's
blessed Virgin Lucy, but in Spring is his home-faring day to
the kingdom of heaven.

32. Now was before told, though less fitly than briefly, about
the uptaking, probation, and enshrinement of the sacred relics
of the blessed Earl Magnus, and not less of the fixing of his
festival. And it is to be remembered and recorded that with
sundry privileges does the Lord God honour his beloved friends
because of their righteousness, some here immediately in this
life, but others after life. Yet seem those dignities among the
saints, somewhat special and surpassing, which belong to
God's martyr Magnus. That is to say, that when his bone was
proved at home in the Orkneys, it turned into the most
beautiful cross in the eyes of the men who were present. Of
this same is another example, that this same bone-cross was
afterwards turned into the most brilliant gold colour even
before the Lord Pope himself at Rome. Wherefore he receives
this purple martyr into the Catalogue of Saints; but that has
been granted to few others in these Northern lands, that he himself [the Pope] has done this. Therefore may we behold and
wonder, though none may conceive it as it is, how abundant is
God Almighty in His riches and in the depths of His mercy: for
He grants these gifts of love to some of His friends, which He
grants not to others, and divides them among them as He
wills; and He fails none, though He gives the gifts of the
Holy Spirit to each of them. Therefore be His name ever
praised and blessed throughout the ages. Amen.

33. From that time were spread abroad and celebrated the
miracles of the holy Earl Magnus over all the western and

---

* The narrative of the Greater Saga is here resumed.

northern parts of the world, and men fared from neighbouring lands, burghs and towns, castles and districts, with great hearts and offering hands, to seek his holy relics, and some sent presents to his sacred shrine, to his honour but for their own healing and salvation, both in this world and in the next. Therefore shall here be told some miracles, though but a few, from the countless number which God granted because of his merits :—

34. When Bergfinn, the franklin north in Shetland, who was named before in this history, heard the joyful tidings of the translation of the holy Earl Magnus, he fared a second time south from Shetland with his leprous son, named Halfdan, to Kirkwall ; and watched, both father and son, at the sacred relics of Earl Magnus. And the holy man of God appeared to Halfdan and passed his hands over his body and at once fell from him all his leprosy. Then he rose up healed. Earl S. Magnus also appeared to the franklin Bergfinn in a dream and said to him : " Now shalt thou receive clear sight, for hither hast thou now come with a true faith and didst not distrust my sanctity, and didst offer to me fair vows, both in prayers and offerings." Then he made the sign of the Cross over Bergfinn's eyes ; and he awaked seeing as well as when he had been sharpest sighted. And father and son both fared home healed, praising God and the holy Earl Magnus.

A man, hight Thorkell, who dwelt in the Orkneys, fell off his barley-rick and was maimed all over one side when he came to the ground. He was borne to the holy Earl Magnus and received there the speedy healing of his hurt, so that his broken bones grew together again and his body was made strong. He thanked God and the holy Earl Magnus for his healing gift.

A man, called Amundi, son of Illugi, a franklin north in Shetland, was a leper and very sick. He fared to the holy Earl Magnus and watched at his shrine and prayed for mercy and healing. As he slept Magnus Earl of the Isles appeared to him and passed his hands over his body and gave him so speedy a cure that he awoke quite whole ; and gave he to God thanks for his healing and to the gracious Magnus.

A man, hight Sigurd, Tandri's son, dwelt in Shetland at the farm called Dale. He became mad, so that he was sewn up in hide. This man was carried to the holy Earl Magnus and got there his senses and complete health, and fared thence sound and whole, praising God and the holy Earl Magnus.

Another man, also hight Sigurd, north in Shetland, had his hands so twisted that all the fingers lay in the palm. He sought the sacred relics of the holy Earl Magnus and received there healing, with straightness and suppleness of his fingers for all his needs. Thanked he God for the mercy which He had granted him for the merits of Earl Magnus.

A man called Thorbiorn Olaf's son, north in Shetland, was witless and possessed of a devil. He was taken to the place of the holy Earl Magnus, and was there at once made whole, and fared back to his house rejoicing and praising God and this blessed martyr.

Thord, who was surnamed Dreka-Skolptr (Dragon-Snout), was hireling to the aforenamed franklin Bergfinn. He was threshing corn in the barley barn on the day before the mass-day of the holy Earl Magnus. But about 3 o'clock in the afternoon Bergfinn bade him leave off work. "It is very seldom," said Thord, "that it seems to thee that too much has been done." Bergfinn said: "The festival which falls to-morrow ought to be kept with all the honour we may and can." Bergfinn then went away, but Thord worked on as before. When a little while was passed, Bergfinn went out again and said to Thord in great anger: "It is the greatest offence to me that thou workest at holy times. Leave off at once on the spot." The franklin went away very wroth, but Thord went on working as before. But when men had nearly done eating, in came Thord in his working clothes and began at once to drink greedily. When he had drunk one horn of ale, he became mad, so that the men had at once to bind him with bonds and that continued for six days. Then the franklin Bergfinn promised for him to give half a mark of silver at the shrine of the holy Earl Magnus, and to let Thord watch there three nights if he might be made whole. Thord was at once healed the next night after the promise had been made for him. And all praised the Highest King of Heaven and his beloved friend the holy Earl Magnus.

It is also said that two men broke gold off from the shrine of the holy Earl Magnus ; one was a Caithness man, the other an Orkneyman. He of Caithness was lost and drowned in the Pentland Firth, and was hight Gilli. The Orkneyman went mad and told in his ravings what they had done. Then was a promise made for him of a pilgrimage to Rome if he were made whole. Afterwards he was taken to the holy Earl Magnus, and a vow was made to him for his recovery, and he became whole at once, and praised God and the holy Earl Magnus.

There was a man called Asmund. On his head fell a great tree and broke all his skull, but the oft-named franklin Bergfinn made a vow for him ; and lots were cast whether there should be promised for him a pilgrimage to Rome or an offering to the Church of Magnus. And the lot came up that he should visit the sacred relics of the holy Earl Magnus. He obtained at once the use of his tongue which he had before lost. He fared then after that to the holy Earl Magnus and watched there and obtained a complete cure of all his hurts. And the franklin Bergfinn gave to Earl Magnus half a mark of silver weighed as he had promised.

There was a woman called Sigrid ; she was the daughter of Sigurd of Sand north in Shetland. She was blind from tender babyhood until she was twenty. Her father took her south to Orkney and let her watch at the shrine of Earl S. Magnus. He offered there a great present. Sigrid received then clear sight in both eyes, and they fared thence, father and daughter, rejoicing and praising God and the holy Earl Magnus.

There was another woman also called Sigrid, daughter of Arnfrid, from the farmstead called Unst north in Shetland. Her leg was broken in twain, and she was taken to the holy Earl Magnus ; and was quickly cured, and thanked God and the holy Earl Magnus.

A third woman also called Sigrid from Unst north in Shetland, was working with the franklin hight Thorlak who lived at Bollastede (Batlasta). Sigrid was sewing in the evening before the mass-day of the holy Earl Magnus after others were keeping the festival. Thorlak enquired why she worked so long, and she answered she would stop. The franklin went out, but she sewed as before. Then came Thorlak again to her and said : " Why doest thou so wrongly at so holy a time ? Now go away and work no longer in my house." She made light of the offence, and then went on sewing as before till it was dark night. But when the men were getting ready to eat, Sigrid became mad so that she had at once to be put in bonds and was grievously possessed, till Thorlak made a promise for her and lots were cast, whether she should fare to Rome or give goods to Earl Magnus. And the lot was thrown that she should go to Kirkwall to the sacred relics of the holy Earl Magnus. Afterwards she was taken thither and got there a wonderful gift of healing of her madness ; and she praised God and his exalted knight Earl Magnus, nevertheless she afterwards fared to Rome for her salvation.

A woman called Groa, from Hrossey, was possessed by an evil spirit and fared to Kirkwall to the holy Earl Magnus, and got there a good cure, and praised God and the holy Earl Magnus.

There was a woman named Ragnhild ; she became a cripple when she was four winters old and all up till she was twenty, then watched she three nights at the holy relics of the Earl S. Magnus. On the third night there appeared to her in her sleep a man bright and glorious, and splendidly clad, and said to her : " Long and often hast thou lain here, great is thy need, rise up now and be made whole and take this staff in thine hand." After that he vanished from her. But she wakened ; she was then holding on to the lock that was on the aumbry on the other side of the Magnus choir. Rose she then up at once completely healed, as if she had never been crippled, with sound bones and sinews, praising God and the holy Earl Magnus. She was with the bishop many winters.

Asa was the name of a woman who had all her days been a cripple. She obtained so excellent a cure from the blessed

Earl Magnus, that she went to Rome that same summer she was healed.

Gudrun was the name of a woman ; she was a cripple for a long time. She obtained a speedy cure of her maimness and a complete cure through the merit and intercession of the holy Earl Magnus, and praised God and his beloved Earl Magnus.

There was a man called Sigurd. He was alms-man at Knot-Sand. He was so very decrepit that he crept on his knees and could not stand upright. He was cured at the shrine of Earl Magnus. He praised God and the holy Magnus.

Two Southerners cast dice for money—one lost a hundred marks. Then was lost all his wealth, except one cog he had left. He then staked the cog against every thing he had lost. Then he who won before, threw two sixes. But for his help the other made a vow to the holy Earl Magnus, that he might get back the rest of his property. After that he threw, and turned up six on one dice, but the other sprang asunder in two parts, and there were seven spots on the two together and thirteen on the three ; and so he won back all his wealth.

35. It happened in Norway, in the days of Harold Gilli, that some rich men and distinguished gave out that two brothers intended to beguile their kinswomen. But the accusation was not true. All the same, the two rich men attacked them, and took them captive, carrying them away from others into a wood, and slew the one of whom they had the greater suspicion. Afterwards they took the other and gave him many and hard tortures with much cruelty, insomuch that they brake in sunder both his legs and as well his arms. After this these cruel men put out both his eyes, therewith cutting his tongue away out of his head, and in such inhuman wise leaving him, they went away ; but he lay there half dead. As soon as they were away, leapt out from the woods many wolves, riving and tearing the flesh from the bones of him who was slain, faring after back into the wood. But of him who was wounded it is to be told that though he could not pray with his tongue for pity, he continually bethought him that Almighty God would grant him some help. Especially did his mind turn there where the holy Earl Magnus was, for at that time

was flourishing most of all his miracle-working. And when
he had made a vow, he became aware that a man was come
to him who was stroking his broken arms and legs. Therewith he takes the short part of his tongue and brings it to
its place at last ; he then lays his hand on the sockets of his
eyes. And with this handling came a wonderful change ; the
eyes took their places with clear vision, the tongue immediately becomes framed for all kinds of speech, the broken
limbs were healed, and all his former health restored. He
sees standing by him a man of fair countenance, with whom
he spake, saying : "What is thy name, noble lord?" The
resplendent man answers : "Here is Earl Magnus, but take
good heed to perform that which thou hast promised to the
Lord." At this he became joyful, and spake thus to him again :
"Since, exalted friend of God, thou hast granted to me a great
gift of healing, I beseech also of thy clemency to intercede with
God for my brother's life." After he had thus spoken, the holy
Magnus vanished away from his sight without answering to
his prayer. But he fell down and thanked God for the mercy
vouchsafed to himself, intending to bide in that place two
nights in steadfast prayer for the help of his brother. And as
the time wore on he looks round, and sees a great pack of
wolves run from the wood to where the corpse lay, and spew
up there all they had eaten of his flesh and bones, and turn
again to the wood. And when a little time was passed, he
sees S. Magnus come, and bless with his right hand all the
wolves' vomit and the bones ; then next to this the body becomes all sound. S. Magnus blesses again his lifeless body,
wherefore he rises up whole and living who before was slain,
and goes to his brother. Greeted then each of them the
other, giving thanks to God and the holy Magnus for so marvellous a mercy as had been granted them. So also let all
hearing such miracles, give manifold praise to the true God,
who grants such wonderful things to sinful men because of
the prayers and merits of his own best beloved friends.

19.* There was a trusty franklin in Westray, called Gunni.
He dreamt that the holy Earl Magnus came to him and said :

---

* This and the following chapters are from the Lesser Saga.

"This shalt thou say to Bishop William, that I would fare out of Birsay east to Kirkwall, and I trust that God will there grant me of His mercy that those who seek me there with a true faith may be healed of their pains. Thou shalt tell thy dream boldly." But when he awoke, he did not dare to tell the dream, because he feared the wrath of Earl Paul. The following night Earl Magnus appeared to him and bade him tell the dream when many were by : " But if thou dost not do so, thou shalt suffer punishment in this world and more in the next." And when he awoke he was filled with fear and fared to Hrossey to see the bishop, and tells the dream at the bishop's mass in a great crowd of men. Earl Paul was there, and all the people prayed the bishop to bear the sacred relics to Kirkwall as Earl Magnus had shown. But Earl Paul stood by silent, and turned blood red. After that fared Bishop William east to Kirkwall with a noble retinue and bore thither the sacred relics of Earl Magnus. The shrine was set over the altar in the Church which is there. There was then at Kirkwall but a trading village with few houses, but it has since greatly increased. Many men have since fared thither and watched there in the Church at the holy relics and have been healed if they vowed to Earl Magnus with true faith.

20. When Earl Rognvald Kali, sister's son to Earl S. Magnus, had come to rule in the Orkneys, and was quietly seated, he caused the ground-plan of the Magnus Church in Kirkwall to be marked out, and got workmen for it, and the work went on well and swiftly ; and it is a noble work and well finished. Afterwards were the sacred relics of Earl Magnus flitted thither, and many signs were wrought there at his holy relics. There is now also a bishop's see which was before at Christ's Kirk in Birsay.

A man, called Eldjarn, the son of Vardi, had a wife and many children, and lived north in Kelduhverf. But during a bad season he became poor and sick, so that he could not help himself, and so little strength had he that he was unable to walk and was driven about among the homesteads. It fell after Easter in spring that he had been driven about on Thursday, Friday, and Saturday, and had had no food. He came at nones on Saturday to where the priest lived and was there through the night. In the morning when men fared to matins, he prayed that he might be taken to the Church ; and it was done. After the matins men fared indoors between the services. But he lay out of doors there where his bed was made : he was so feeble that he thought he was about to die. It came also into his mind how he had been before his poverty when he had his property all together, and his prayer which he prayed, touched him so much that he was greatly moved. Then he took and promised a six days' fast, if God would give him some relief : this fast he vowed both before S. Olaf's and S. Magnus' day. When he had uttered his vow, men came to the service and the priest sang mass. When the Epistle was read he fell asleep, but those who were beside him thought he was about to die. In his sleep a vision passed before him, in which he thought he saw a great light within the choir, and that it came out to him. He saw with the light a beautiful man, and he said to him: " Eldjarn! hast thou little strength now ? " He thought he answered : " So methinks, though perhaps it may not be so. But who art thou?" He answers : " I am Earl S. Magnus, Erlend's son. Wilt thou be made whole?" He answers : " I will." He replied : " King S. Olaf also has heard thy prayer and the vow which thou hast made to us two for thy healing. But he sent me hither to give thee healing : for a woman made a vow to him west in the Firths, and he has fared thither to make her whole." Then began Earl Magnus to pass his hands over him, but he woke up when the Gospel was begun. He asked the men who stood nearest him to lift him up. But they answered : " Why should we lift thee up, when thou hast no strength?" He replies : " I think I am now cured." They took him and raised him on to his feet, and he stood all through the Gospel and so on to the end of the mass. After mass he went in to the priest and tells the miracle, how God had given him healing. And all praised God for the mercy which He had granted to him for the merit of Earl S. Magnus. May he obtain for us mercy and pardon for our sins from our Lord Jesus Christ, who, with the Father and the Holy Spirit, liveth and reigneth God for ever and ever. Amen.

Also published
by Llanerch:

MEDIAEVAL CHRONICLES OF SCOTLAND:
THE CHRONICLES OF MELROSE
AND HOLYROOD

TWO CELTIC SAINTS:
THE LIVES OF NINIAN AND KENTIGERN
by Ailred and Joceline

SYMBOLISM OF THE CELTIC CROSS
by Derek Bryce

LIVES OF THE BRITISH SAINTS
by Baring-Gould and Fisher

ARTHUR AND THE BRITONS
IN WALES AND SCOTLAND
by W. F. Skene

THE MYSTICAL WAY
AND THE ARTHURIAN QUEST
by Derek Bryce

THE CELTIC LEGEND
OF THE BEYOND.
by Anatole Le Braz

From booksellers.
For a complete list,
write to:
LLANERCH ENTERPRISES,
Felinfach, Lampeter,
Dyfed, Wales,
SA48 8PJ.